ROSÉ
COCKTAILS

A COLLECTION OF 50
REFRESHING COCKTAILS

EMANUELE MENSAH

CIDER MILL
PRESS

BOOK
PUBLISHERS

13-Digit ISBN: 978-1-95151-137-1
10-Digit ISBN: 1-951511-37-9

This book may be ordered by mail from the publisher. Please include $5.99 for postage and handling. Please support your local bookseller first!

Books published by Cider Mill Press Book Publishers are available at special discounts for bulk purchases in the United States by corporations, institutions, and other organizations. For more information, please contact the publisher.

Cider Mill Press Book Publishers
"Where good books are ready for press"
501 Nelson Place
Nashville, Tennessee 37214

cidermillpress.com

Typography: Gotham, Adobe Caslon, and Eveleth Clean Thin

Printed in Malaysia

23 24 25 26 27 TJM 6 5 4 3 2

CONTENTS

INTRODUCTION

Rosé is for ladies. False. Rosé is made from red and white grapes. False. Rosé is just a summer wine. And false again.

If you believe that all of these statements are true, then it is time for you to immerse yourself in a new world—the rosé one.

Whether you call it *rosé* (French), *rosado* (Spanish), or *rosato* (Italian), you are about to find out a huge quantity of information about rosé that you could never imagine.

I like to think of rosé as an iceberg. What people usually know about it is just the tip of the iceberg, but truth be told, there is a lot more.

Until a few years ago, I was one of those people who totally snubbed rosé, thinking it was too girlish or that it would be useless as a mixing ingredient for a cocktail. But I had to change my mind and acknowledge the different opportunities that rosé can offer, not only in terms of wine.

For sure, everybody knows how well it goes with food. How great it is in summer. But do you know that it can make fantastic cocktails too?

If you fancy a glass of rosé before dinner or are one of those people who think rosé is not a wine, please join me in this new journey to discover the versatility of a wine that, until a few years ago, was not so popular.

Let me introduce you to its history and characteristics; let's look at the different types and categories. Then, together, we will see and understand how it is made and what are the best ways to drink it. And finally, let me transport you to a world of unique cocktails that will change your perspective and make you fall in love with rosé.

Take a seat, grab a glass of wine—rosé in this case—and relax. Welcome to the darker side of rosé.

PART ONE:
ALL ABOUT ROSÉ

WHAT IS ROSÉ?

As already said, rosé is not a blend of white and red grapes. Rather, rosé is a type of wine made from red wine grapes, and, to be precise, it can be made from nearly any red grape cultivated in any wine-growing region. The difference between rosé and red stays in the fermenting process: while red wine ferments with the grape's skin intact for weeks and months, rosé stays in contact with the skin only for a few hours, and that's how it gets its pink color.

Rosé is a French word meaning pink and, as per the wine's name, its origins are to be situated in Provence, France, where the majority of rosé in the world is produced. Provence is a southeastern region of France, bordered by the Rhône River and Languedoc to the west, by Italy to the east, and by the Mediterranean Sea to the south.

But as mentioned already, rosé can be produced anywhere, such as in California, Italy, and Spain. Rosés produced in Europe are typically very dry, while those produced in the New World tend to be sweeter and fruitier.

ROSÉ—THE OLDEST AMONG THE WINES?

Although rosé wine rose to fame only a few years ago, its origins can be dated back to ancient Greece, where blends of white and red grapes were diluted with water. At that time, rosé was a pink juice, slightly off-dry and tannic. Eventually, Greeks (and Romans as well) learned to separate grapes, so red and white wines were born.

In the sixth century, the Phocaeans brought grape vines from Greece to Marseille (Massalia back at the time), where they started their production of red and white grape blends. Soon the pink wines became popular around the Mediterranean, and southern France became the epicenter of rosé wine.

Despite the development of new techniques to press wine, rosé was still preferred, and it still was during the Middle Ages, when a pink wine called claret began to be produced in Bordeaux.

Claret was quite popular until the late 1900s, while for most of the 20th century, the rosé wine industry was dominated by two Portuguese wine producers, Mateus and Lancers. Then, after a period of decline early in the 21st century, rosé wine gained its popularity again.

ROSÉS FROM AROUND THE WORLD

Since rosé can be made from any type of grape, there is a vast selection on the market. So it's quite impossible to list them all, but let's see the most famous producers together.

Of course, the first one is Provence, in France, considered the native land of rosé. Provence has nine *Appellations d'origine contrôlée* (AOC) and the *Côte de Provence* is the largest. Rosés are typically made with grenache, cinsault, syrah, and mourvèdre grapes, and they are light-bodied and refreshing. Tibouren grapes, which grow in Provence, are often used to make full-bodied rosé with a distinctive earthy, floral, and berry-like aroma.

Another French region famous for its rosé production is the Rhône Valley, where wines made with cabernet franc and pinot noir grapes tend to be earthy and slightly fruity. On the other end, the Loire Valley produces refreshing rosé with high acidity and low alcohol content.

Italy has several *Denominazione d'origine controllata*. Examples are: *Chiaretto* that identify pale-colored wine with an intense minerality and zesty acidity; *Ramato*, made in Veneto, are copper-colored wines due to an extended maceration of pink-skinned pinot grigio; *Cerasuolo* has a vivid rosé color and takes its name from the cherries (*cirasce* in the Abruzzo dialect), and *Premetta*, a type of rosé that keep its very pale color even after an extended maceration.

Spain's rosés are known as *rosados*, and they are produced throughout the country. In some regions, deeper pink wines are knowns as *claretes*, and they were traditionally made from red and white grapes with a partial contact with the skin during the fermentation. However, today rosado is the only legally recognized term and can identify both a short maceration and a direct press method.

Northern California is famous for its viticultural areas and for the production of white zinfandel. They do not produce only sweet rosés, but also dry. California rosés are light and fresh. On the other hand, in Washington state, rosés have a crispy acidity and herbal and mineral notes.

New Zealand's rosés can be robust and spicy, such as the one in Hawke's Bay using merlot or syrah, or can be intense and have stone fruits flavors, such as the one in the Marlborough District.

TYPES OF ROSÉS

DRY AND SWEET, THE TWO MAIN CATEGORIES

Like red and white wines, rosé can be dry and sweet.

Dry rosés are the most common and the most produced around the world; they are usually drier in the Old World than in the New World. Dry rosés are low in sugar, high in tannins, and have more acidity and an intense fruit flavor as well.

Sweet rosés are obtained by not fermenting the fruit sugars into alcohol so that the juice will have fewer tannins (which increases the dryness in wines).

According to the grapes used, you may be able to understand if the rosé you bought will be dry or sweet. Just keep in mind that the sweetness of a rosé often depends on the winemaker's choice.

THE VARIETIES OF GRAPES

Since rosé can be made with almost any type of grape, it's quite challenging to list them all. Moreover, they can be made from only one variety, or a blend of two or three grape varieties. But let's review the most common ones.

We can split the varieties of grapes accordingly into the two main categories we saw above. That's because, depending on the variety used, the wine will be more or less sweet.

Starting with the dry wines, some of the grapes used are:

Grenache grapes from Spain

Tempranillo grapes from Spain

- **Grenache**: this is the predominant grape used in Provence, and it is often blended with syrah and cabernet sauvignon grapes. Rosés made with grenache are among the driest in the world and, in terms of flavor, they have red fruits flavor with a zesty finish. They do have floral notes, too, and are often full-bodied. Grenache, alongside cinsault, is one of the main grapes used in **Tavel**, a wine-growing *Appellations d'origine contrôlée (AOC)* in the southern Rhône region. Tavel AOC wines tend to have more body than most of the rosés.

- **Cinsault**: used throughout the Languedoc and southern Rhône, these rosés have a floral aroma.

- **Pinot noir**: rosés made with pinot noir grapes have earthy notes and tend to be bright and acidic. They do have fruity flavors as well, such as strawberry and melon. They are delicate on the palate and have a dry finish. Pinot noir grapes are often used to make rosé Champagne.

- **Syrah**: rosés made from syrah have a deep color and a boisterous profile.

Grenache grapes from Spain   *Tempranillo grapes from Spain*

They are very tannic, bold, and rich, with a pleasantly dry finish. Syrah rosés have plum, cherry, and strawberry notes, with a hint of black pepper.

- **Mourvèdre**: light in color, Mourvèdre rosés are full-bodied and have red fruit and floral notes. Rosés are not aged (they are produced for their freshness and fruitiness), but rosés made with mourvèdre grapes (which are known for their ageability) are often aged, giving high quality. These types of rosés can be aged for up to ten years.

- **Sangiovese**: this grape is originally from Italy, but nowadays it's grown all over the world. Sangiovese rosés are bold, with red fruits notes and a hint of spice.

- **Tempranillo**: a Spanish variety that makes savory and dry rosé. They have a spicy and earthy quality, with crispy, fruity notes. The wine is usually pale to medium pink.

- **Cabernet Sauvignon**: cab sauv rosés are dry and more acidic than regular cabernet sauvignon wines. They usually range from tangy citrus notes to touches of tobacco and leather.

When we talk about sweet rosé wine, instead, we talk mainly about three types of wines:

- **White zinfandel**: made with zinfandel grapes, it's a sweet and bright pink rosé created accidentally by stuck fermentation at Sutter Home Winery in California back in the 1970s, using black zinfandel grapes (they were actually trying to make a more intense and deeper zinfandel). It's considered a blush wine.

- **White merlot**: starting to be produced in the 1990s as an alternative to white zinfandel, white merlot, which is made with merlot grapes, is sweet and fruity. Like its counterpart, it's often labeled as a blush wine.

- **Pink moscato**: this is a type of wine made from muscat blanc grape with a dash of red wine, typically merlot, in order to add some color and make it pink. It can be still or sparkling, and it's often served as a dessert wine.

SPARKLING ROSÉ VERSUS ROSÉ CHAMPAGNE

There is a great variety of sparkling rosés on the market due to the different grapes used and the production method. Generally speaking, sweet sparkling rosés have fruity-tasting notes, such as raspberry and strawberry, while dry sparkling rosés have a sharper flavor, such as grapefruit and rhubarb.

Popular varieties of sparkling rosés are: *Cava*, a Spanish wine made with Macabeu grapes (but grenache and pinot noir as well); *Sekt*, a German-style of rosé which is less sweet than Champagne; and *prosecco rosé*, hailing from Italy and made with 85% of Glera grapes and 10%–15% of pinot noir and left to be fermented in stainless steel tanks for at least 60 days.

Rosé Champagne can be only made in the French region of Champagne, where the pigmentation is usually achieved by adding red wine (pinot noir, in most cases, or pinot meunier) to the blend. Another method consists of removing the pink juice from the must at an early stage and then fermenting without the skin (saignée method, page 18). Typically rosé Champagne has a red fruit aroma and is often dry.

PRODUCTION PROCESS

HOW ROSÉ IS MADE

There are three main ways to make rosé wine: maceration (or skin contact), saignée (or bleed), and blending.

The maceration method

It is the most common way, and it's when red wine grapes are pressed and then left to rest (macerate) in their own skins from anywhere from around two to twenty-four hours; after that, the skins are removed in order to ensure the color, flavor, and tannins. The longer the skin is left, the darker the rosé will be. Next, the juice resulting from the maceration undergoes a shorter fermentation, and finally, it is pressed to remove any traces of grape skin and then bottled.

The saignée method

From French "to bleed," the saignée method is relatively rare due to its process. In the early stages of making red wine, some of the juice is bled off and put in a different vat so that the red wine will be more intense in flavor and in color and, at the same time, a rosé will be produced. In this case, rosés are a byproduct of red wine and closer to it in terms of flavor.

The blending method

It is not only uncommon but also unpopular. In fact, in the European Union, blending is prohibited by the European Commission; it is allowed only in the French region of Champagne to make rosé Champagne. The method consists of adding a little bit of red wine to a vat of white wine in post-fermentation. Still rosés made with the blending method are labeled as blush (see next page).

Other methods of making rosés

The **decolorization method** involves the decolorization of red wine. It uses activated carbon to absorb the color and flavor of the wine at a high rate. To do so, the red wine is passed through a charcoal filter system until it gets the desired shade of pink. Since aromas and flavors are absorbed, this process is never used to produce high-quality rosés.

The **vin gris method** (or direct pressing method), from French "grey wine," consists of pressing the grapes right away (no maceration time) in order to remove the skin and avoid too much contact with it. As a result, rosés produced with this method are the lightest in color.

BLUSH WINES

Rosé and blush are terms often used interchangeably, but there is a slight difference between them. If rosés go through a maceration process or a saignée one, blush refers both to a wine undergoing the maceration or a direct processing method and the blending method. Blush wine can be made in a palette of colors, from light to medium pink.

The term "blush" originated in the 1970s in the United States to name a pale and pinkish wine made from cabernet sauvignon grapes. But since back then white wines were extremely popular, blush style wines were affiliated with the term "white" or "blanc."

HOW TO DRINK ROSÉ

FLAVOR PROFILE

As we already know at this point, rosés are made with a huge variety of grapes; therefore, based on that, each wine will be different, ranging from savory to dry to sweet. In general, rosés resemble a light red wine flavor profile, but they are brighter and crisper. They are fresh and fruity. Light rosé is pink and has strawberry, grapefruit, or mint flavor. Light-medium rosés are just a bit darker than light rosés and have more of an herbal and floral flavor profile. Medium rosés start to turn into a darker pink and have raspberry, hibiscus, or white pepper flavor. Full rosés are quite dark pink and have berry, bell pepper, or black pepper notes.

SHADES OF ROSÉ

Let's start by saying that you can't always rely on the color to identify a rosé. For example, not all dark rosés are sweet, nor are all pink ones dry. The shade

of pink doesn't correlate to its sweetness. As mentioned previously, the color depends on the length of time the juice is left to rest with the skin of the grape, alongside the type of grape used.

In 2004, the **Centre de Recherche et d'Expérimentation sur le Vin Rosé** in Vidauban displayed a panel of nine colors to describe rosés: red currant, onion peel, brick, raspberry, flesh, rosewood, salmon, pink marble, and coral. But some of the color names were not adapted for the market; therefore, the **Conseil Interprofessionnel des Vins de Provence (CIVP)**, which represents more than 600 wine producers and forty trade companies in France, worked alongside the Centre de Recherche to modify the classifications. The panel of the color changed in: peach, melon, lychee, grapefruit, mango, raspberry, apricot, mandarin, and red currant. But, always for marketing reasons, the CIVP dropped the number of colors from nine to six, changing some names too. The final result is: mandarin, mango, melon (cantaloupe), peach, pomelo (grapefruit), and red currant.

GLASSWARE

If red wines are served in a large round bowl (to increase the oxidation) and white wines in a smaller bowl, with rosés, we can be more flexible. The most common is a stemmed glass with a short bowl and a slight taper or flared lip. If the wine is dry, go for the tapered bowl; if it's sweet and fruity, go for the flared one because it will help to concentrate the wine on the part of the tongue most sensitive to sweetness.

TEMPERATURE AND DECANTING

Like white wines, rosés are best served chilled. The correct temperature is between 50°F and 60°F (10°C–15°C). Just place your favorite rosé in the fridge a couple of hours before serving it, and that will do. Try to avoid ice cubes

because they will dilute and change the flavor of the wine. And if you have just a glass, remember to place the rosé back in the fridge. Most rosés will last up to three days (sometimes up to five days, so always check before throwing it away).

Rosés rarely need to be decanted, but if they do, it's usually not more than thirty minutes before serving the wine. Decanting is good practice when the wine shows signs of reduction (excessive sulfur compounds). If you decant a rosé, just remember that it needs to be very cold because the decanting process will likely raise the temperate and, as previously mentioned, rosés need to be served chilled to be enjoyed at their best.

AGING

Rosés are not aged wines; that's because they are produced especially for their freshness, youthfulness, and fruity taste. Moreover, even if rosés have a high acidity that is suitable for storing wines, they mostly don't have the structure to support the wine once the acidity falls flat.

There is an exception. Rosés produced in the Bandol wine region in Provence are known for their aging potential and complexity. In Bandol, to produce rosés, they use the mourvèdre grape which is known for its agebility. When mourvèdre is incorporated into a rosé (usually blended with grenache and cinsault), the ageability passes on.

FOOD PAIRING

Rosés can be paired with a wide range of cuisine and flavor profiles thanks to the wide variety of grapes that can be used to make this surprising wine.

My recommendation is to dig a little bit into the characteristics of the grape so that you will know more about the rosé you are drinking and the best way to pair it with food.

General rule of thumb is that lighter rosés will pair better with delicate food, such as salads or seafood, while full-bodied rosés match well with BBQ meat or spicy food.

TOOLS AND INGREDIENTS: HOW TO ALWAYS BE READY

When making wine-based cocktails, there are a few essential tools you will need in order to make a perfect drink.

Let's take a look at the essential tools you need to have to serve and preserve the wine at its best.

WINE OPENER

This is the first tool you are going to need whether you just want to have a glass of wine or if you want to make yourself a cocktail. Believe it or not, you can find any type of wine opener on the market. The **waiter's corkscrew** is one of the most common due to its simplicity and portability. The **wing corkscrew** is one of the oldest types, yet not so popular because it requires you to apply more force compared to the modern ones. **Electric wine openers** are very easy to use—a good choice for a beginner. The **ah-so cork puller** is quite small and can be easily stored or carried. As with the wing corkscrew, this one also requires a certain amount of strength. Then we have the **air pressure pump** that allows us to open a bottle by using air pressure to push the cork out of the bottle. The **lever corkscrew** is an easy one to use: just push down the lever and pull it back. The **twist-and-pull corkscrew** is easy to use but requires some effort; that's

why it's not one of the most popular. The **legacy corkscrew** is one of the most expensive and is usually popular among wine collectors. It needs to be attached to a table and can open bottles faster than many other types of wine openers. The **Durand** is a new style of opener, quite expensive, and ideal for older and fragile corks.

These are just examples, but there is a vast selection of wine openers on the market; you just need to find the one that's perfect for you.

BOTTLE STOPPERS AND WINE PRESERVER

While you want to aerate your wine when you open it, when you close the bottle, you need to cut off the oxygen so that you will be able to preserve the wine. If you can reuse the original cork, then do it; otherwise, it's always good to have some bottle stoppers. As with wine openers, you can also find a good selection of stoppers on the market; some of them preserve the wine for a couple of days, and others allow the wine to stay fresh for up to two weeks. The most common ones are natural corks with plastic tops and silicone stoppers. But you can find **decorative stoppers** as well, generally a steel cork with a rubber or cork stopper with a decorative pull at the top to make it easy to remove it from the bottle. Even if they seal out the air, they still allow some oxidation to continue, and therefore they extend a wine's life for only a day or two. **Pour stoppers** allow you to seal the bottle and pour the wine through a small spout in order to minimize the spillage. They are made of metal or plastic and extend a wine's life for a day or two. **Vacuum preservation stoppers** allow you to preserve a wine for about two weeks. They work alongside a pump (some of them can do the job without a pump): the rubberized stopper is placed on the bottle, and then a manual or battery pump removes the oxygen out of the open bottle.

Another type of wine preservation system is represented by the **Coravin**, an opener that allows you to preserve the wine without opening the bottle. It uses a needle to insert through the cork and fills the bottle with argon gas that will replace the lost wine and preserve what is left.

You can often use a wine stopper (not the pump, though) for Champagne and sparkling wines too, but **sparkling wine bottle stoppers** work best. Most sparkling wine stoppers have two wings that you need to clamp down over the bottle. Others expand inside the bottle to create a seal, and some others use the pressure generated by the Champagne or sparkling wine to create a tight seal on the bottle. Keep in mind that sparkling wine won't last more than three days (very few stoppers allow a longer lifespan); they do lose their carbonation quickly once opened.

BUCKETS

A bucket chiller is the best solution for when you have a gathering or dinner party. Just fill the bucket with a mixture of ice and water, and your wine will stay chilled. This is also the most affordable solution; others include stylish and sophisticated coolers or bottle sleeves that eliminate the messy drips that a traditional ice bucket would cause.

ESSENTIAL BAR TOOLS

The bartending world is characterized by a great number of tools, which sometimes make the job easier and sometimes just make it funnier.

But if you are a beginner or want to always be ready to make a cocktail at home, then the following are the must-haves or at least the ones that you are going to need to make the cocktails listed in the following chapters.

A **shaker** is one of the first tools to buy when approaching the bartending world for the first time. True, but also false. The purpose of the shaker is to introduce air bubbles to the drink in order to give it the right texture and temperature. You can use any type of vessel with a tight seal, such as a protein shaker, but I would recommend you buy one if you are interested in improving your skills.

Then you will need a **strainer**, so you will be able to separate the ice used to shake or stir from the drink itself, and a **jigger**, the most reliable way to measure the liquids. But do not worry, if you don't have a jigger, you can always use a spoon or a cup.

Then a **spoon, knife,** and a **chopping board**. You can use a regular spoon, but you will find it easier to mix a cocktail with a **barspoon**. They have a spiral handle, a shallow bowl, and are longer than regular spoons. A knife and chopping board are a must if you want to improve your garnish skills. Get a small, light knife; it will allow you more control, and you will be able to make fancy garnishes.

And finally, you are going to need a **mixing glass** (or large tin or shaker) to control the texture and dilution of the cocktails, and a **blender** to make fantastic frosé (frozen rosé—see page 79).

ESSENTIAL INGREDIENTS

Fruits, herbs, flowers. Here comes the creative part of making a cocktail. Of course, you don't need to have all sorts of ingredients at home; just a few will do. In fact, several excellent cocktails can be made with only two or three ingredients.

I've always pictured rosé as a summery and refreshing wine, perfect for long hot days. So I have focused on ingredients that highlight it and create a delicious triumph of flavors. **Strawberries, mangos,** and **raspberries** are first in line. But do not forget the citrus—they are our big allies when it comes to making a cocktail. We always have a **lemon** or an **orange** at home. Just a few drops, or added as a garnish, will give the right balance to your cocktail. Then you have fresh **mint** and all sorts of **herbs and spices** to work with. Not only are some of them a great match to rosés, but they also make beautiful garnishes. And finally, **edible flowers** are always a nice touch, making your cocktails look gorgeous.

PART TWO: THE COCKTAIL RECIPES

RECIPES
USING
DRY ROSÉ

APPLE & SAFFRON SPRITZ

Tasting notes: fruity, zesty, sweet

A very balanced low-ABV cocktail, perfect for an aperitif with friends. The beautiful yellow bright color and the saffron honey flavor will bring you straight to spring. Beautiful, intense, and delicious.

YIELD: 1 COCKTAIL

---

1 ⅔ ounces (50 ml) apple skin-infused dry rosé wine (see page 134)

⅔ ounce (20 ml) lemon juice

1 ½ tablespoon (30 ml) saffron honey (see page 165)

Mediterranean tonic water

1 edible petal flower

(1) Fill a mixing glass or a metal shaking tin with ice.

(2) Pour apple skin-infused dry rosé wine, lemon juice, and saffron honey into the chilled vessel, and stir rapidly with a barspoon for 17 to 20 seconds.

(3) Strain into a chilled flute.

(4) Top up with Mediterranean tonic water and garnish with an edible petal flower.

Bartender's Tips: *Get the Granny Smith for this recipe. It has a stronger citrus note, and is more refreshing. Or you can play with different types of apples. You will have a slightly different flavor with each type, so choose the one that you like the most.*

FRUITY BEETS

Tasting notes: fruity, tropical, fizzy

A bright and tropical cocktail, an all-day drink. It's low ABV, refreshing, and full of flavors.

YIELD: 1 COCKTAIL

½ ounce (15 ml) dry rosé wine

½ ounce (15 ml) bourbon

½ ounce (15 ml) Aperol

½ ounce (15 ml) lemon juice

⅓ ounce (10 ml) pineapple juice

1 barspoon (5 ml) simple syrup 2:1 (see page 166)

Sparkling rosé

1 beet (beetroot) cracker

(1) Combine dry rosé wine, bourbon, Aperol, lemon juice, pineapple juice, and simple syrup 2:1 in a small metal shaker tin.

(2) Fill with ice cubes to the top and close the shaker. Hard shake for 10 seconds until the shaker is frozen.

(3) Double strain into a chilled Nick-and-Nora glass.

(4) Top up with sparkling rosé.

(5) Garnish with a beet cracker.

Bartender's Tips: You can find beet crackers in-store, and they give an extra kick to this cocktail. If you can't find them, choose a savory appetizer to complement this drink, such as spiced nuts or other savory crackers—a great combination.

GIMLÉ

Tasting notes: sour, refreshing, sweet

A little twist on a classic Gimlet, this cocktail is more for those who fancy sweet cocktails. Great for hot summer days when you want to spend more time outside and less inside. Just grab these three ingredients, and the jeux sont faits!

YIELD: 1 COCKTAIL

1 ⅔ ounces (50 ml) gin

⅔ ounce (20 ml) lime juice

⅔ ounces (20 ml) dry rosé wine syrup (see page 163)

(1) Combine gin, lime juice, and dry rosé wine syrup in a small metal shaker tin.

(2) Fill with ice cubes to the top and close the shaker. Hard shake for 10 seconds until the shaker is frozen.

(3) Double strain into a chilled coupette.

PALOMITO

Tasting notes: smoked, spiced, fizzy

A lovely and refreshing drink with spiced notes from ginger and a touch of smoking flavor. If you like a classic Paloma, this is a spiced version of it.

YIELD: 1 COCKTAIL

---

1 ounce (30 ml) dry rosé wine

¾ ounce (25 ml) mescal

⅓ ounce (10 ml) lime juice

⅔ ounce (20 ml) grapefruit juice

⅓ ounce (10 ml) ginger syrup
(see page 154)

1 barspoon (5 ml) simple syrup
2:1 (see page 166)

Ginger ale

1 grapefruit slice

(1) Combine dry rosé wine, mescal, lime juice, grapefruit juice, ginger syrup, and simple syrup 2:1 in a small metal shaker tin.

(2) Fill with ice cubes to the top and close the shaker. Hard shake for 10 seconds until the shaker is frozen.

(3) Double strain into a chilled highball over a block of ice.

(4) Garnish with a grapefruit slice.

Bartender's Tips: Go for a sangiovese rosé wine: red fruits notes and a spiced flavor are a great pairing for mescal and ginger, linking all together in a wonderful highball.

PASSIONY

Tasting notes: tropical, sour, fizzy

A whiskey highball twist, with hints of passion fruit and citrus. A very refreshing summer cocktail with layers of sweetness, fruit, and smoke.

YIELD: 1 COCKTAIL

---

1 ounce (30 ml) passion fruit-infused dry rosé (see page 139)

1 ⅓ ounces (40 ml) blend scotch whiskey

⅓ ounce (10 ml) lemon juice

⅓ ounce (10 ml) simple syrup 2:1 (see page 166)

Soda water

½ passion fruit

(1) Fill a mixing glass or a metal shaking tin with ice.

(2) Pour passion fruit-infused dry rosé, blend scotch whiskey, lemon juice, and simple syrup 2:1 into the chilled vessel, and stir rapidly with a barspoon for 17 to 20 seconds.

(3) Strain into a chilled highball over a cube of ice.

(4) Top up with soda water and garnish with half a passion fruit.

RED GLASS ON A HIGHWAY

Tasting notes: fruity, sweet, refreshing

A delightful cocktail to have instead of a dessert or as a boozy slush. Whether you drink it in the afternoon or in the evening, it will be great.

YIELD: 10 COCKTAILS

---

3 cups (400 g) fresh strawberries

1 bottle dry rosé wine

3 ⅓ ounces (100 ml) Aperol

3 ⅓ ounces (100 ml) lime juice

2 ⅓ ounces (70 ml) strawberries syrup (see page 167)

1 or 2 basil leaves

(1) Blend dry rosé wine, Aperol, strawberries, lime juice, and strawberries syrup at high speed.

(2) Place in a bowl and store in the freezer for up to 12 hours.

(3) Blend again until you get a smooth texture.

(4) Pour into a chilled coupette with the help of a spoon.

(5) Garnish with one or two basil leaves.

Bartender's Tips: *Go for a full-bodied rosé wine, such as grenache or mourvèdre, as they will keep their strong characteristics.*

ROSÉ-GHITA

Tasting notes: citrus, fruity, dry

A twist on a classic margarita with some fruity notes from the Aperol and a bit of tannin from the dry rosé. A refreshing cocktail that makes an excellent aperitif.

YIELD: 1 COCKTAIL

¾ ounce (25 ml) dry rosé wine

1 ⅓ ounces (40 ml) tequila

½ ounce (15 ml) Aperol

⅔ ounce (20 ml) lime juice

¼ ounce (7.5 ml) simple syrup 2:1 (see page 166)

Pinch of salt

(1) Combine dry rosé wine, tequila, Aperol, lime juice, and simple syrup 2:1 in a small metal shaker tin.

(2) Fill with ice cubes to the top and close the shaker. Hard shake for 10 seconds until the shaker is frozen.

(3) Double strain into a chilled rocks glass over a block of ice.

(4) Garnish with salt on the rim.

Salt that rim! *To rim the glass, take a lime wedge and pass the pulp over the glass's rim until the whole perimeter is moist. Grab the glass from the base or the stem and, upside down, let it rest in a shallow saucer where you put salt. Rotate the glass until the whole rim is coated. It's easy, and you get a nice and simple garnish for your cocktail.*

ROSÉ & MELON FIZZ

Tasting notes: herbal, refreshing, fruity

Picture yourself on one of those long and hot summer days when you need something refreshing and thirst-quenching. Here Rosé & Melon Fizz comes, a delicious combination of flavors that will give you a break from the hot temperatures.

YIELD: 1 COCKTAIL

---

1 ⅙ ounces (35 ml) dry rosé wine

⅔ ounce (20 ml) fennel seeds-infused tequila (see page 137)

1 barspoon (5 ml) lemon juice

⅓ ounce (10 ml) melon juice (see page 148)

⅖ ounce (12.5 ml) vanilla syrup (see page 171)

Soda water

1 melon slice

(1) In a jar, combine dry rosé wine, fennel seeds-infused tequila, lemon juice, melon juice, and vanilla syrup.

(2) Pour the liquid into a soda siphon and fill it with CO_2. Store it in the fridge for 3 hours before serving cocktails.

(3) Pour the sparkling liquid from the siphon into a chilled highball over ice.

(4) Top up with soda water and garnish with a melon slice.

(5) Store the rest of the juice mixture in the fridge for up to 2 weeks or until it is fizzy.

Go juicy! *If you want to make a mocktail out of Rosé & Melon Fizz, remove the alcoholic parts and adjust the rest of the ingredients: ⅔ ounce (20 ml) lemon juice, 1 ⅔ ounces (20 ml) melon juice, ⅔ ounce (20 ml) vanilla syrup. Top up with lemonade instead of soda water.*

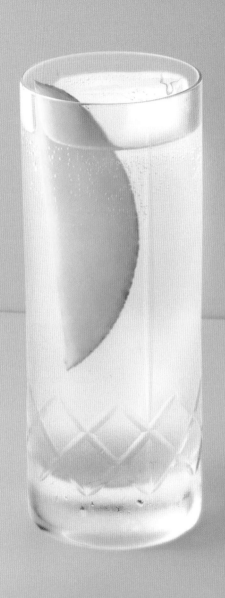

ROSEBERRY ROMANCE

Tasting notes: nutty, fruity, sour

A Clover Club-style of drink that offers you extra layers of flavors: from the sweetness of the raspberries to the citrus notes to the texture given from the egg white. A new discovery for your palate!

YIELD: 1 COCKTAIL

⅔ ounce (20 ml) raspberries-infused dry rosé (see page 140)

1 ounce (30 ml) gin

¾ ounce (25 ml) lemon juice

½ ounce (15 ml) toasted pine nuts syrup (see page 169)

¾ ounce (25 ml) egg white

1 lemon wedge

(1) Combine raspberries-infused dry rosé, gin, lemon juice, toasted pine nuts syrup, and egg white in a small metal shaker tin.

(2) Fill with ice cubes to the top and close the shaker. Hard shake for 10 seconds until the shaker is frozen.

(3) Double strain into a chilled rocks glass over a block of ice.

(4) Garnish with a lemon wedge.

Bartender's Tips: *I recommend a pinot noir rosé wine to add flavor to the cocktail; a bit earthy with a dry finish that will pair well with gin and toasted pine nuts syrup.*

ROSMANGO FIZZ

Tasting notes: tropical, citrus, fizzy

A fantastic mango-based cocktail with floral and citrus notes. This cocktail will transport you straight away to the Caribbean.

YIELD: 1 COCKTAIL

---

1 ⅓ ounces (40 ml) dry rosé wine

1 ounce (30 ml) white rum

⅓ ounce (10 ml) lime juice

Mango soda (see page 173)

1 mango slice

(1) Fill and chill a mixing glass or a metal shaking tin with ice.

(2) Pour dry rosé wine, white rum, and lime juice into the vessel and stir rapidly with a barspoon for 17 to 20 seconds.

(3) Strain into a chilled highball over ice.

(4) Top up with mango soda.

(5) Garnish with a mango slice.

Soft Mango Fizz: *Make a soft drink version for your kids. It's delicious, and they are going to love it. Just remove the alcoholic part of the cocktail and balance it with simple syrup 2:1 to your taste.*

ROSÉ FOUNTAIN

Tasting notes: fruity, fizzy, sweet

A fruity punch bowl to share during your summer parties. Match it with Mediterranean food—Rosé Fountain will surprise you.

YIELD: 10 COCKTAILS

5 ounces (150 ml) dry rosé wine

5 ounces (150 ml) tequila

5 ounces (150 ml) lime juice

3 ⅓ ounces (100 ml) cranberry juice

6 ⅔ ounces (200 ml) raspberry syrup (see page 159)

1 cup (200 ml) soda

1 raspberry

(1) Pour dry rosé wine, tequila, lime juice, cranberry juice, and raspberry juice into a punch bowl.

(2) Top up with soda.

(3) Add ice cubes and garnish each cup with a raspberry.

Bartender's Tips: I recommend adding ice cubes at the end in order for the drink to be well mixed.

This punch bowl is perfect for house parties. Just make it in advance so you have more time to entertain your guests.

ROSÉ JUNGLE BIRD

Tasting notes: fruity, bitter, sour

Inspired by a classic Jungle Bird, the spiced rosé wine is my way to replicate the spiced notes that you can find in a dark rum, but with a low ABV.

YIELD: 1 COCKTAIL

---

1 ⅔ ounces (50 ml) spiced dry rosé wine (see page 141)

½ ounce (15 ml) Campari

⅔ ounce (20 ml) lime juice

½ ounce (15 ml) pineapple juice

⅓ ounce (10 ml) simple syrup 2:1 (see page 166)

2 dashes Angostura bitters

3 pineapple leaves

(1) Combine dry spiced rosé wine, Campari, lime juice, pineapple juice, simple syrup 2:1, and Angostura bitters in a small metal shaker tin.

(2) Fill with ice cubes to the top and close the shaker. Hard shake for 10 seconds until the shaker is frozen.

(3) Double strain into a tiki mug and fill it with crushed ice.

(4) Garnish with 3 pineapple leaves and a straw.

ROSÉ SMASH

Tasting notes: floral, sour, dry

A twist on a Southside with basil instead of mint and the addition of rosé wine. A very refreshing drink for this summer.

YIELD: 1 COCKTAIL

---

4 basil leaves

¾ ounce (25 ml) dry rosé wine

1 ⅓ ounces (40 ml) gin, such as Bayab Dry

⅓ ounce (10 ml) lemon juice

⅓ ounce (10 ml) simple syrup 2:1 (see page 166)

1 basil leaf

(1) Combine basil leaves, dry rosé wine, gin, lemon juice, and simple syrup 2:1 in a small metal shaker tin.

(2) Fill with ice cubes to the top and close the shaker. Hard shake for 10 seconds until the shaker is frozen.

(3) Double strain into a chilled rocks glass over a block of ice.

(4) Garnish with a basil leaf.

Bartender's Tips: *A dry, fruity and zesty rosé wine will be a good match for Rosé Smash and will play well with a dry gin, such as Bayab Dry. Bayab Dry is a West African gin with refreshing and citrusy notes that will give an extra kick to the cocktail.*

STARRY FLOWER

Tasting notes: fizzy, floral, sweet

A low-ABV cocktail with an intense floral note. Starry Flower is bight and refreshing; it shouts "Summer!" out loud.

YIELD: 1 COCKTAIL

---

2 ⅓ ounces (70 ml) dry rosé wine

1 barspoon (5 ml) Suze

⅓ ounce (10 ml) lemon juice

½ ounce (15 ml) star fruit cordial (See page 131)

Elderflower tonic

1 star fruit slice

(1) Fill a mixing glass or a metal shaking tin with ice.

(2) Pour dry rosé wine, Suze, lemon juice, and star fruit cordial into the chilled vessel, and stir rapidly with a barspoon for 17 to 20 seconds.

(3) Strain into a chilled highball over a block of ice.

(4) Top up with elderflower tonic and garnish with a slice of star fruit.

Bartender's Tips: I recommend a dry rosé made with Tempranillo grapes: their earthy notes with a crispy, fruity flavor work perfectly in this highball.

WALNUT & PLUM HIGHBALL

Tasting notes: nutty, sweet, sparkling

A bright highball with complex nutty and fruity notes. Walnut & Plum Highball is a very well-balanced sweet-and-sour cocktail, rich and intense.

YIELD: 1 COCKTAIL

---

1 ⅓ ounces (40 ml) dry rosé wine

⅔ ounce (20 ml) toasted walnut-infused whiskey (see page 145)

⅖ ounce (12.5 ml) honey water (see page 156)

⅓ ounce (10 ml) lemon juice

Plum soda (see page 174)

1 plum wheel

(1) Fill and chill a mixing glass or a metal shaking tin with ice.

(2) Pour dry rosé wine, toasted walnut-infused whiskey, honey water, and lemon juice into the vessel and stir rapidly with a barspoon for 17 to 20 seconds.

(3) Strain into a chilled highball over ice.

(4) Top up with plum soda.

(5) Garnish with a plum wheel.

Bartender's Tips: If you use ice cubes, add the soda first and then the ice. This way, the drink will be mixed better.

SUMMER GARDEN N.1

Tasting notes: refreshing, fruity, sweet

A very delicate cocktail with a hint of watermelon; a real treat for those who love a long drink and fruity taste.

YIELD: 1 COCKTAIL

---

1 ⅓ ounce (40 ml) dry rosé wine

⅔ ounce (20 ml) lime juice

1 ⅓ ounce (40 ml) watermelon juice

⅔ ounce (20 ml) rosemary syrup (see page 164)

Ginger ale

1 rosemary sprig

(1) Combine dry rosé wine, lime juice, watermelon juice, and rosemary syrup in a small metal shaker tin.

(2) Fill with ice cubes to the top and close the shaker. Hard shake for 10 seconds until the shaker is frozen.

(3) Double strain into a chilled highball over a block of ice.

(4) Garnish with a rosemary sprig.

Bartender's Tips: *Go for a grenache rosé wine—they have a fantastic, versatile profile: fruity and floral notes, which are a great match for Summer Garden N.1, and with a zesty hint that recalls the acidic part of the cocktail.*

TROPICAL ARRIVAL

Tasting notes: citrus, sweet, fruity

If you fancy a passion fruit martini, you will love Tropical Arrival too. It's a low-ABV cocktail with tropical flavor that will transport you to a paradise island. Grab a magazine and sunglasses and sip away.

YIELD: 1 COCKTAIL

---

1 ⅓ ounces (40 ml) dry rosé wine

⅔ ounce (20 ml) vodka

½ ounce (15 ml) Cointreau

½ ounce (15 ml) lime juice

½ ounce (15 ml) simple syrup 2:1 (see page 166)

⅔ ounce (20 ml) mango puree, store-bought

1 mango slice

(1) Combine dry rosé wine, vodka, Cointreau, lime juice, simple syrup 2:1, and mango puree in a small metal shaker tin.

(2) Fill with ice cubes to the top and close the shaker. Hard shake for 10 seconds until the shaker is frozen.

(3) Double strain into a chilled coupette.

(4) Garnish with a mango slice.

Bartender's Tips: *Go for a Shiraz rosé wine that, with its berry and spiced notes and clean, crisp finish, goes well with Tropical Arrival. Sip with Mexican food—it will be a delicious combination.*

TROPICAL ROSÉ RAIN

Tasting notes: fruity, tropical, sweet

A refreshing low-ABV cocktail with tropical fruits notes combined with the freshness of coriander seeds. A triumph of flavor that will explode in your mouth.

YIELD: 1 COCKTAIL

¾ **ounce (25 ml) toasted coriander seeds-infused dry rosé (see page 143)**

⅔ **ounce (20 ml) white rum**

⅔ **ounce (20 ml) lemon juice**

⅔ **ounce (20 ml) pineapple juice**

1 barspoon (5 ml) passion fruit syrup (see page 157)

⅓ **ounce (10 ml) witbier (white ale) reduction (see page 172)**

1 passion fruit slice

(1) Combine toasted coriander seeds-infused dry rosé, white rum, lemon juice, pineapple juice, passion fruit syrup, and witbier reduction in a small metal shaker tin.

(2) Fill with ice cubes to the top and close the shaker. Hard shake for 10 seconds until the shaker is frozen.

(3) Double strain into a chilled rocks glass over a block of ice.

(4) Garnish with a slice of passion fruit.

RECIPES
USING
SWEET ROSÉ

APPLE ROSÉ MARTINI

Tasting notes: fruity, sour, sweet

A sour drink with a low ABV; apple juice brings sweetness to the drink and makes it refreshing.

YIELD: 1 COCKTAIL

---

1 ⅓ ounces (40 ml) sweet rosé wine

¾ ounce (25 ml) vodka

⅔ ounce (20 ml) lemon juice

1 ounce (30 ml) apple juice

½ ounce (15 ml) simple syrup 2:1 (see page 166)

Apple coin

(1) Combine sweet rosé wine, vodka, lemon juice, apple juice, and simple syrup 2:1 in a small metal shaker tin.

(2) Fill with ice cubes to the top and close the shaker. Hard shake for 10 seconds until the shaker is frozen.

(3) Double strain into a chilled coupette.

(4) Garnish with an apple coin.

CLEMENTÉ SODA

Tasting notes: sweet, fruity, sparkling

A very refreshing flute to drink with your friends. Bright, light, and delicious.

YIELD: 1 COCKTAIL

¾ ounce (25 ml) sweet rosé wine

1 ounce (30 ml) gin

⅓ ounce (10 ml) lime juice

1 barspoon (5 ml) grenadine (see page 155)

Clementine tonic water

(1) Fill a mixing glass or a metal shaking tin with ice.

(2) Pour sweet rosé wine, gin, lime juice, and grenadine into the chilled vessel, and stir rapidly with a barspoon for 17 to 20 seconds.

(3) Strain into a chilled flute.

(4) Top up with clementine tonic water.

Bartender's Tips: *Clementé Soda is a low-ABV, light cocktail. Clementines add a little bit of bitterness. Drink it as an aperitif.*

CUCUMBER & ROSÉ HIGHBALL

Tasting notes: sour, fizzy, refreshing

A Gin Sour–style cocktail with cucumber flavor that adds freshness, and elderflower tonic that brings a floral note.

YIELD: 1 COCKTAIL

½ ounce (15 ml) sweet rosé wine

1 ⅔ ounces (50 ml) gin

⅔ ounce (20 ml) lemon juice

½ ounce (15 ml) cucumber syrup (see page 153)

Elderflower tonic

1 cucumber slice

(1) Combine sweet rosé wine, gin, lemon juice, and cucumber syrup in a small metal shaker tin.

(2) Fill with ice cubes to the top and close the shaker. Hard shake for 10 seconds until the shaker is frozen.

(3) Double strain into a chilled highball over a block of ice.

(4) Top up with elderflower tonic.

(5) Garnish with a cucumber slice.

Soft Highball: A twist on a London Calling with cucumber, rosé, and elderflower tonic instead of soda, the Cucumber & Rosé Highball is a very refreshing cocktail that can be made as a mocktail, too. Remove the alcoholic part and combine 1 ⅔ ounces (50 ml) cucumber syrup with 3 ⅓ ounces (100 ml) soda in a highball. A simple and tasty soft drink for your kids!

FRUITY BAG

Tasting notes: sweet, fizzy, fruity

A fruity highball with a Mediterranean touch from the blood orange. A real treat for those who love sweet cocktails.

YIELD: 1 COCKTAIL

---

1 ⅓ ounces (40 ml) vodka

⅔ ounce (20 ml) sweet rosé and strawberry syrup (see page 168)

Blood orange tonic water

1 strawberry

(1) Fill a mixing glass or a metal shaking tin with ice.

(2) Pour vodka and sweet rosé and strawberry syrup into the chilled vessel, and stir rapidly with a barspoon for 17 to 20 seconds.

(3) Strain into a chilled highball over ice.

(4) Top up with blood orange tonic water.

(5) Garnish with a strawberry.

Vodka Sour: Combine 1 ⅔ ounces (50 ml) vodka, ¾ ounce (25 ml) lemon juice, ½ ounce (15 ml) sweet rosé and strawberry syrup, and ¾ ounce (25 ml) egg white. Shake it, and you will get a sour, fruity cocktail to serve to your guests. If you like a sour style of drink, this is a nice twist.

LABIRINTO

Tasting notes: sweet, sour, dry

A bourbon-based cocktail with a touch of rosé that adds tannin and brightness. If you have a sweet tooth, you will love this one. Have it instead of a dessert—it will stay in your mouth for a while, giving you a pleasant end to your dinner.

YIELD: 1 COCKTAIL

---

1 ounce (30 ml) bourbon

¾ ounce (25 ml) lemon juice

⅓ ounce (10 ml) sweet rosé wine syrup (see page 163)

1 barspoon (5 ml) grenadine (see page 155)

⅔ ounce (20 ml) egg white

2 dashes Peychaud's Bitters

1 edible flower

(1) Combine bourbon, lemon juice, sweet rosé wine syrup, grenadine, egg white, and Peychaud's Bitters in a small metal shaker tin.

(2) Fill with ice cubes to the top and close the shaker. Hard shake for 10 seconds until the shaker is frozen.

(3) Double strain into a chilled coupette.

(4) Garnish with an edible flower.

Bartender's Tips: Rosé syrup is versatile and works in many drinks, and it's also a great way to use leftover wine. Rosé syrup will add sweet and tart notes. Try it with some classic cocktails, and you will never waste leftover wine again!

LYCHEE ROSÉ MARTINI

Tasting notes: fruity, sweet, tropical

An intense lychee note matched with the sweetness of rosé makes this cocktail quite tasty. The presence of grenadine also brightens and highlights the rosé wine.

YIELD: 1 COCKTAIL

---

1 ⅓ ounces (40 ml) sweet rosé wine

⅔ ounce (20 ml) white rum

1 barspoon (5 ml) lemon juice

⅔ ounce (20 ml) lychee juice

⅓ ounce (10 ml) grenadine (see page 155)

1 orange peel

(1) Fill a mixing glass or a metal shaking tin with ice.

(2) Pour sweet rosé wine, white rum, lemon juice, lychee juice, and grenadine into the chilled vessel, and stir rapidly with a barspoon for 17 to 20 seconds.

(3) Strain into a coupette.

(4) Garnish with an orange peel.

MANGO ESSENCE FROSÉ

Tasting notes: fruity, tropical, citrus

A frosé (frozen rosé) is an all-time favorite and very refreshing summer cocktail. It's great for garden parties. The mango adds lots of tropical notes and sweetness.

YIELD: 10 COCKTAILS

10 ounces (300 ml) sweet rosé wine

3 ⅓ ounces (100 ml) vodka

3 ⅓ ounces (100 ml) lime juice

6 ⅔ ounces (200 ml) mango puree, store-bought

3 ⅓ ounces (100 ml) simple syrup 2:1 (see page 166)

(1) Blend sweet rosé wine, vodka, lime juice, mango puree, and simple syrup 2:1 at high speed.

(2) Place mixture in a bowl and store it in a freezer for up to 12 hours.

(3) Blend it again until you get a smooth texture.

(4) Pour into a chilled coupette with the help of a spoon.

(5) If you like, garnish with a mango slice.

Mangossert! You can make a mocktail version of the Mango Essence Frosé so your kids will be able to enjoy it as a snack or dessert. Just remove rosé wine and vodka, and you will have a delicious granita-style mocktail!

PEACH & COCOA WISHER

Tasting notes: smoke, sweet, citrus

Let yourself be enrapt by the intense flavor of the bourbon, the floral notes of the rosé syrup, and the fruitiness of the roasted peach. A fantastic cocktail that will accompany you throughout the summer.

YIELD: 1 COCKTAIL

---

1 ⅓ ounces (40 ml) vanilla pods-infused bourbon (see page 146)

⅓ ounce (10 ml) crème de cacao blanc

⅔ ounce (20 ml) lime juice

½ ounce (15 ml) sweet rosé wine and roasted peach syrup (see page 162)

1 mint sprig

(1) Pour vanilla pods-infused bourbon, crème de cacao blanc, lime juice, sweet rosé wine, and roasted peach syrup into a shaker.

(2) Combine crushed ice and churn.

(3) Pour in a chilled highball and finish it with more crushed ice.

(4) Garnish with a mint sprig and a straw.

Bartender's Tips: This rich and spiced cocktail has chocolate and caramelized peach notes. Try it as an after-dinner cocktail—you will love it!

PEACHY ROSÉ SOUR

Tasting notes: sweet, fruity, sour

Although it's made with a sweet rosé, Peachy Rosé Sour is not actually that sweet. This is a great example of how you can turn your ingredients upside down and give them a new connection. Just because white zinfandel is known as sweet rosé, it doesn't mean that it can't make a fantastic sour cocktail. Plus, it can be enjoyed by those who don't have a sweet tooth. It's a win-win.

YIELD: 1 COCKTAIL

1 ounce (30 ml) white zinfandel

1 ounce (30 ml) vodka

½ ounce (15 ml) lemon juice

½ ounce (15 ml) simple syrup 2:1 (see page 166)

⅔ ounce (20 ml) peach puree (see page 150)

⅔ ounce (25 ml) egg white

3 dashes Angostura bitters

(1) Combine white zinfandel, vodka, lemon juice, simple syrup 2:1, peach puree, and egg white in a small metal shaker tin.

(2) Fill with ice cubes to the top and close the shaker. Hard shake for 10 seconds until the shaker is frozen.

(3) Double strain into a chilled coupette.

(4) Garnish with three dashes of Angostura bitters.

Bellini Twists: *If you have enough peach puree left, just add 1 ⅔ ounces (50 ml) of it to 3 ⅓ ounces (100 ml) of sparkling rosé, ⅖ ounce (12.5 ml) lemon juice, and ⅓ ounce (10 ml) simple syrup 2:1 to get a twist on a Bellini.*

PLUM ROSÉ

Tasting notes: sweet, fruity, dry

A summer drink with fruity notes from the plums, and an intense flavor of rosé that matches very well with agave. I recommend giving a hard and strong shake, as in a daiquiri style of shake. And do not forget to eat the plum soaked in the drink—it will be delicious!

YIELD: 1 COCKTAIL

---

1 ounce (30 ml) gin

¾ ounce (25 ml) lemon juice

⅔ ounce (20 ml) plum juice

½ ounce (15 ml) agave

½ ounce (15 ml) sweet rosé reduction (see page 161)

1 plum wheel

(1) Fill a mixing glass or a metal shaking tin with ice.

(2) Pour gin, lemon juice, plum juice, agave, and sweet rosé reduction into the chilled vessel, and stir rapidly with a barspoon for 17 to 20 seconds.

(3) Strain into a chilled rocks glass over a block of ice.

(4) Garnish with a plum wheel.

Bartender's Tips: *Go for Bayab Dry gin to highlight the citrusy notes of the drink.*

Seedlip for mocktails: *If you want to make a mocktail version, you can use 1 ½ ounces (45 ml) Seedlip, a nonalcoholic spirit, instead of gin. Then just remove the sweet rosé reduction, and you will have a nice soft drink for the summer.*

RASPBERRY ROSÉ COLLINS

Tasting notes: fruity, sour, fizzy

Delicious and easy to make, this vodka-and-raspberry sour needs a hard shake to break the raspberries. Then, once shaken, top it up with soda that will brighten the flavors.

YIELD: 1 COCKTAIL

4 raspberries

1 ounce (30 ml) sweet rosé wine

1 ounce (30 ml) vodka

¾ ounce (25 ml) lime juice

½ ounce (15 ml) simple syrup 2:1

1 ⅔ ounces (50 ml) soda water

1 lime wedge

1 mint sprig

(1) Combine raspberries, sweet rosé wine, vodka, lime juice, and simple syrup 2:1 in a small metal shaker tin.

(2) Fill with ice cubes to the top and close the shaker. Hard shake for 10 seconds until the shaker is frozen.

(3) Double strain into a chilled highball over a block of ice.

(4) Top up with soda water and garnish with a lime wedge and a mint sprig.

Bartender's Tips: *Choose a sweet rosé, such as a white merlot, because it will add fruity red notes such as raspberry, which elevate the fruitiness of the cocktail.*

ROSÉ ATTRACTION

Tasting notes: nutty, fruity, sour

A delicious and fruity cocktail that will let you look at kiwi in a new way. Use gold kiwis, as they add a hint of sweetness to the drink.

YIELD: 1 COCKTAIL

---

1 ⅓ ounce (40 ml) toasted almond flour-infused tequila (see page 144)

⅔ ounce (25 ml) lime juice

⅔ ounce (25 ml) kiwi juice

½ ounce (15 ml) sweet rosé wine syrup (see page 163)

3 dashes celery bitters

1 kiwi slice

(1) Combine toasted almond flour-infused tequila, lime juice, kiwi juice, sweet rosé wine syrup, and celery bitters in a small metal shaker tin.

(2) Fill with ice cubes to the top and close the shaker. Hard shake for 10 seconds until the shaker is frozen.

(3) Double strain into a chilled rocks glass over a block of ice.

(4) Garnish with a kiwi slice.

ROSÉ CRUSH

Tasting notes: fruity, earthy, spicy

An unusual pairing of ingredients, this drink is like a summer garden—a concoction of flavors that will blow your mind.

YIELD: 1 COCKTAIL

---

1 ⅓ ounces (40 ml) sweet rosé wine

¾ ounce (25 ml) fava beans-infused vodka (see page 136)

⅓ ounce (10 ml) lime juice

1 ounce (30 ml) watermelon juice

½ ounce (15 ml) simple syrup 2:1 (see page 166)

4 drops chili tincture (see page 152)

1 grapefruit wedge

1 mint sprig

(1) In a chilled rocks glass, pour sweet rosé wine, fava beans-infused vodka, lime juice, watermelon juice, simple syrup 2:1, and chili tincture.

(2) Half fill the glass with crushed ice and churn the drink with a barspoon.

(3) Top up with more crushed ice and churn again.

(4) Repeat the process so the drink fills the cup and frost forms on the outside. Once you build the drink, let the cup get frosty. This could take at least 20 to 25 seconds or up to 1 minute.

(5) Slap the mint sprig with your hands to release its aromatic oils. Garnish the cocktail with a grapefruit slice and one mint sprig.

ROSÉ MARTINEZ

Tasting notes: sweet, dry, tannin

A twist on the Martinez that is part sweet rosé and part sweet vermouth, adding a bit of complexity to the cocktail.

YIELD: 1 COCKTAIL

¼ ounce (7.5 ml) sweet rosé

1 ⅓ ounces (40 ml) gin

¼ ounce (7.5 ml) sweet vermouth

1 dash Angostura bitters

1 dash orange bitters

1 orange peel

(1) Fill a mixing glass or a metal shaking tin with ice.

(2) Pour sweet rosé, gin, sweet vermouth, Angostura bitters, and orange bitters into the chilled vessel, and stir rapidly with a barspoon for 17 to 20 seconds.

(3) Strain into a chilled coupette.

(4) Garnish with an orange peel.

Bartender's Tips: *I recommend using a white merlot rosé that will add fruity notes and sweetness to the cocktail. Those who don't particularly like Martinez because it's too strong will be able to appreciate Rosé Martinez.*

ROSÉ PENICILLIN

Tasting notes: sweet, smoke, sour

A twist on a Penicillin, with a touch of rosé honey that makes the cocktail sweet but spiced at the same time, thanks to the presence of ginger juice.

YIELD: 1 COCKTAIL

---

1 ounce (30 ml) scotch whiskey

⅔ ounce (20 ml) blend whiskey

⅔ ounce (20 ml) lemon juice

⅓ ounce (10 ml) ginger juice (see page 147)

⅓ ounce (10 ml) sweet rosé honey (see page 160)

1 lemon wedge

(1) Combine scotch whiskey, blend whiskey, lemon juice, ginger juice, and sweet rosé honey in a small metal shaker tin.

(2) Fill with ice cubes to the top and close the shaker. Hard shake for 10 seconds until the shaker is frozen.

(3) Double strain into a chilled rocks glass over a block of ice.

(4) Garnish with a lemon wedge.

ROSÉ PISCO SOUR

Tasting notes: sour, sweet, earthy

A twist on a Pisco Sour, very smooth and with nice texture and body. Give it a try!

YIELD: 1 COCKTAIL

---

1 ⅔ ounces (50 ml) pisco

¾ ounce (25 ml) lime juice

½ ounce (15 ml) pineapple juice

⅔ ounce (20 ml) sweet rosé honey (see page 160)

¾ ounce (25 ml) egg white

2 drops Angostura bitters

(1) Combine pisco, lime juice, pineapple juice, sweet rosé honey, egg white, and Angostura bitters in a small metal shaker tin.

(2) Fill with ice cubes to the top and close the shaker. Hard shake for 10 seconds until the shaker is frozen.

(3) Double strain into a chilled coupette.

Bartender's Tips: *Instead of egg white, you can add three drops of vegan foam to your cocktail to make a fantastic foam. That way, can still enjoy Rosé Pisco Sour even if you have an egg allergy. Ms. Better's Bitters Miraculous Foamer is available online.*

ROSÉ ROOTS

Tasting notes: earthy, sour, sweet

A sour-style drink with some vegetable notes. A very tasty cocktail for a relaxing Sunday afternoon.

YIELD: 1 COCKTAIL

½ ounce (15 ml) sweet rosé wine

1 ounce (30 ml) parsnip-infused white rum (see page 138)

⅔ ounce (20 ml) lime juice

⅔ ounce (20 ml) pomegranate juice

½ ounce (15 ml) thyme syrup (see page 170)

1 raw parsnip ribbon

(1) Combine sweet rosé wine, parsnip-infuse white rum, lime juice, pomegranate juice, and thyme syrup in a small metal shaker tin.

(2) Fill with ice cubes to the top and close the shaker. Hard shake for 10 seconds until the shaker is frozen.

(3) Double strain into a chilled rocks glass over a block of ice.

(4) Garnish with a raw parsnip ribbon.

RUSTY STONE BLOOD

Tasting notes: fruity, zesty, refreshing

Here is your new summer concoction: a delicious, orangey cocktail to accompany your brunches. It's light and refreshing and goes equally well with scones and savory sandwiches. It's one of those drinks that you never want to stop drinking.

YIELD: 1 COCKTAIL

---

1 ⅔ ounces (50 ml) blood orange peels-infused sweet rosé (see page 135)

⅔ ounce (20 ml) apricot liqueur

⅔ ounce (20 ml) lime juice

1 barspoon (5 ml) simple syrup 2:1 (see page 166)

1 dehydrated apricot

(1) Combine blood orange peels-infused sweet rosé, apricot liqueur, lime juice, and simple syrup 2:1 in a small metal shaker tin.

(2) Fill with ice cubes to the top and close the shaker. Hard shake for 10 seconds until the shaker is frozen.

(3) Double strain into a chilled coupette.

(4) Garnish with a dehydrated apricot.

SPICED ROSÉ

Tasting notes: fruity, spiced, sweet

A sour drink with fruity notes from the peach and a delicate flavor from the sweet rosé, all spiced with the ginger fruit—this cocktail will please every palate.

YIELD: 1 COCKTAIL

½ ounce (15 ml) sweet rosé wine

1 ⅓ ounces (40 ml) vodka

⅔ ounce (20 ml) lemon juice

⅓ ounce (10 ml) ginger syrup
(see page 154)

½ ounce (15 ml) peach syrup
(see page 158)

1 ginger candy

(1) Combine sweet rosé wine, vodka, lemon juice, ginger syrup, and peach syrup in a small metal shaker tin.

(2) Fill with ice cubes to the top and close the shaker. Hard shake for 10 seconds until the shaker is frozen.

(3) Double strain into a chilled rocks glass over a block of ice.

(4) Garnish with a ginger candy.

SUNSET FLUTE

Tasting notes: sour, sweet, sparkling

Rhubarb and raspberry are a game-changing combo. Here, the raspberry works really well with the rosé, while the rhubarb complements the gin. The delicious lime cordial adds citrusy sweetness to the cocktail.

YIELD: 1 COCKTAIL

---

1 once (30 ml) sweet rosé wine

¾ ounce (25 ml) gin

½ ounce (15 ml) lime cordial (see page 130)

Rhubarb and raspberry tonic

(1) Fill a mixing glass or a metal shaking tin with ice.

(2) Pour sweet rosé wine, gin, and lime cordial into the chilled vessel, and stir rapidly with a barspoon for 17 to 20 seconds.

(3) Strain into a chilled flute.

(4) Top up with rhubarb and raspberry tonic.

RECIPES USING SPARKLING ROSÉ

BASIL ROSÉ SPRITZ

Tasting notes: earthy, citrus, refreshing

This cocktail will match your afternoon at the park perfectly. Bright and light, it will get you ready for dinner. Basil adds a hint of freshness to the drink—perfect to pair with charcuterie and Mediterranean cheeses.

YIELD: 1 COCKTAIL

6 basil leaves

1 ⅓ ounces (40 ml) gin

⅔ ounce (20 ml) lemon juice

½ ounce (15 ml) tomato cordial
(see page 132)

¾ ounce (25 ml) sparkling rosé

1 lemon coin

(1) Combine basil leaves, gin, lemon juice, and tomato cordial in a small metal shaker tin.

(2) Fill with ice cubes to the top and close the shaker. Hard shake for 10 seconds until the shaker is frozen.

(3) Double strain into a chilled flute.

(4) Top up with sparkling rosé, and give a squeeze of the lemon coin before discarding it.

BLOOD APERITIVO

Tasting notes: fruity, fizzy, sweet

A twist on an Aperol Spritz, but fruitier than the classic version. Sparkling rosé, instead of prosecco, brings a sweet side to the drink.

YIELD: 1 COCKTAIL

---

1 ounce (30 ml) Aperol

1 ⅓ ounce (40 ml) blood-orange juice

Sparkling rosé

1 blood orange wedge

(1) Pour Aperol and blood-orange juice into a chilled wine glass.

(2) Top up with sparkling rosé.

(3) Fill the wine glass with ice cubes.

(4) Garnish with a blood orange wedge.

Bartender's Tips: *Blood oranges are sweeter than other oranges and have a light tartness with a nice berry hint.*

BELLINI IN VACATION

Tasting notes: sweet, fizzy, fruity

A refreshing, easy-to-make cocktail that's perfect for any moment of the day. It's so delicious that one won't be enough.

YIELD: 1 COCKTAIL

---

1 ⅔ ounces (50 ml) watermelon cordial (see page 133)

Sparkling rosé

1 grapefruit coin

(1) Pour watermelon cordial into a chilled flute.

(2) Top up with sparkling rosé.

(3) Gently stir it with a barspoon.

(4) Squeeze a grapefruit coin on top and discard it.

Bartender's Tips: *As in a classic Bellini, go for prosecco rosé. Bubbly, refreshing, and full of flavors, it will add fruity and floral notes to the drink.*

ELDERFLOWER SPRITZ N.3

Tasting notes: sweet, floral, fizzy

A great aperitif cocktail that you can enjoy on the beach. It's so easy to make that you will be able to prepare it anywhere. Just don't forget to bring a cooling bag for the ice and the sparkling rosé.

YIELD: 1 COCKTAIL

---

1 ⅔ ounces (50 ml) elderflower liqueur

⅓ ounce (10 ml) lemon juice

Sparkling rosé

(1) Fill a mixing glass or a metal shaking tin with ice.

(2) Pour elderflower liqueur and lemon juice into the chilled vessel, and stir rapidly with a barspoon for 17 to 20 seconds.

(3) Strain into a chilled wine glass.

(4) Top up with sparkling rosé.

JALISCO SPRITZER

Tasting notes: fruity, citrus, fizzy

A fruity and sour highball with vanilla notes. It will dazzle you with its flavors and aroma. A must-try for the summer.

YIELD: 1 COCKTAIL

---

1 ⅓ ounces (40 ml) raspberries-infused dry rosé (see page 140)

1 ounce (30 ml) tequila

⅓ ounce (10 ml) lemon juice

⅓ ounce (10 ml) vanilla syrup (see page 171)

Sparkling rosé

1 lemon wedge

(1) Pour raspberries-infused dry rosé, tequila, lemon juice, and vanilla syrup into a chilled highball.

(2) Top up with sparkling rosé and add ice.

(3) Garnish with a lemon wedge.

FRENCH ROSÉ COCKTAIL

Tasting notes: dry, sparkling, floral

A little twist on a French 75 with sparkling rosé, making it brighter and fruitier. Grenadine gives more body to the drink, making it jammy.

YIELD: 1 COCKTAIL

---

1 ⅓ ounces (50 ml) pink gin

¾ ounce (25 ml) lemon juice

⅖ ounce (12.5 ml) grenadine
(see page 155)

Sparkling rosé

1 orange coin

(1) Combine pink gin, lemon juice, and grenadine in a small metal shaker tin.

(2) Fill with ice cubes to the top and close the shaker. Hard shake for 10 seconds until the shaker is frozen.

(3) Double strain into a chilled large coupette.

(4) Garnish with an orange coin.

FLOATING LEAF

Tasting notes: fruity, sweet, sparkling

Floating Leaf is light and refreshing. A hint of basil pairs perfectly with the sparkling rosé, creating a delicious cocktail to welcome the summer.

YIELD: 1 COCKTAIL

---

1 ⅓ ounces (40 ml) strawberries-infused vodka (see page 142)

⅔ ounce (20 ml) lemon juice

½ ounce (15 ml) basil syrup (see page 151)

½ ounce (15 ml) sparkling rosé reduction (see page 161)

Soda water

1 basil leaf

(1) Combine strawberries-infused vodka, lemon juice, basil syrup, and sparkling rosé reduction in a jar.

(2) Pour the liquid into a soda siphon and fill it with CO_2. Store it in the fridge for 3 hours before serving cocktails.

(3) Pour the sparkling liquid from the siphon into a large chilled coupette.

(4) Top up with soda water and garnish with a basil leaf.

(5) Store the rest of the juice mixture in the siphon in the fridge for up to 2 weeks or until it is fizzy.

Bartender's Tips: Make more than one Floating Leaf; otherwise, you will waste a soda charger.

HIDDEN SWEET

Tasting notes: sparkling, dry, sweet

Champagne rosé works really well with brown sugar and cognac. The sugar cube will dissolve, giving Hidden Sweet more sweetness. So sip it slowly.

YIELD: 1 COCKTAIL

---

1 brown sugar cube

1 dash Angostura bitters

¾ ounce (25 ml) cognac

3 ounces (90 ml) Champagne rosé

(1) Place a brown sugar cube in a chilled flute, followed by a dash of Angostura bitters.

(2) Pour cognac and top up with Champagne rosé.

Bartender's Tips: *Rosé Champagne is fruitier than Champagne, with red fruits flavors, such as strawberry and cranberry. With its delicate bubbles and crisp and clean finish, it will be a nice addition to the cocktail.*

MELON CHAMPAGNE COCKTAIL

Tasting notes: fizzy, fruity, sweet

A delicious midday cocktail with tropical flavors. Sparkling rosé will add brightness and a delicate note.

YIELD: 1 COCKTAIL

½ ounce (15 ml) lemon juice

⅔ ounce (20 ml) pineapple juice

⅔ ounce (20 ml) simple syrup 2:1 (see page 166)

1 ounce (30 ml) melon puree, store-bought or homemade (see page 149)

Champagne rosé

(1) Fill a mixing glass or a metal shaking tin with ice.

(2) Pour lemon juice, pineapple juice, simple syrup 2:1, and melon puree into the chilled vessel, and stir rapidly with a barspoon for 17 to 20 seconds.

(3) Strain into a chilled flute.

(4) Top up with Champagne rosé.

PINK STRAWBERRY ROSÉ

Tasting notes: sweet, fruity, sparkling

A strawberry highball, very refreshing and great to have after work. The bubbles will make you hungry for dinner.

YIELD: 1 COCKTAIL

¾ ounce (25 ml) gin

⅓ ounce (10 ml) lemon juice

½ ounce (15 ml) strawberries syrup (see page 167)

1 dash orange bitters

3 ⅓ ounces (100 ml) sparkling rosé

Lime wedge

(1) Pour gin, lemon juice, strawberries syrup, and orange bitters into a chilled highball.

(2) Top up with sparkling rosé.

(3) Add ice and garnish with lime wedge.

Bartender's Tips: Add ice as the last step. It will help you mix the ingredients better.

Rossini Twist: If you have some strawberries syrup left, you can make a twist on a classic Rossini. Combine 3 ounces (90 ml) prosecco rosé, ⅔ ounce (20 ml) strawberries syrup, and 1 ⅓ ounces (40 ml) strawberry puree in a rocks glass over ice. Top up with soda water and garnish with a strawberry.

RHUBARB ROSÉ SPRITZ

Tasting notes: fruity, fizzy, sweet

A little twist on an Aperol Spritz made with sparkling rosé. The combination of Aperol and rosé works really well and highlights the original fruity notes of the Aperol.

YIELD: 1 COCKTAIL

---

1 ½ ounces (45 ml) Aperol

1 ⅙ ounces (35 ml) soda water

3 ounces (90 ml) sparkling rosé

1 grapefruit wedge

(1) Pour Aperol, soda water, and sparkling rosé into a chilled highball, then fill with ice.

(2) Garnish with a grapefruit wedge.

Bartender's Tips: A spritz is such a classic summer cocktail, and you can make several twists on it. Swap prosecco with prosecco rosé, and you will already have a slightly different drink. That's not all. Once you have your sparkling part, you can play with it by adding Campari to have a rosé Campari Spritz.

SPICED SUMMER BOWL

Tasting notes: spiced, fruity, sweet

An alternative summer punch bowl drink to share with your friends and family. Sip it during your aperitif parties—success guaranteed.

YIELD: 10 COCKTAILS

---

6 ⅔ ounces (200 ml) lemon juice

6 ⅔ ounces (200 ml) strawberry juice

3 ⅓ ounces (100 ml) ginger syrup (see page 154)

Sparkling rosé

1 strawberry

1 mint sprig

(1) Pour lemon juice, strawberry juice, and ginger syrup into a punch bowl.

(2) Top up with sparkling rosé.

(3) Add ice cubes and garnish each cup with a strawberry and a mint sprig.

Bartender's Tips: *Punch is considered to be the earliest cocktail and is a good balance between spirits, citrus, spice, and sweetness.*

PART THREE: DIY INGREDIENT RECIPES

• CORDIALS •

Cordials can be alcoholic or not. They can be sipped slowly or used in cocktails. Alcoholic cordials contain 30% ABV, and, according to the legal definition, they fall under the same category as liqueurs, which are flavored spirits made with fruits, flowers, juices, plants, or plants extracts. Sometimes the word "cordial" can identify a sweet dessert-like distilled spirit, such as a chocolate liqueur, or, as said at the beginning, a nonalcoholic syrupy drink such as lime cordial.

LIME CORDIAL

Lime cordial is normally used for a classic Gimlet cocktail, but it can be used for many other drinks, such as Sunset Flute (see page 104), and can be infused with spices and herbs in order to add more flavor. It's absolutely delicious with soda as well: combine, in a highball filled with ice, 1 2/3 ounces (50 ml) lime cordial with 3 1/3 (100 ml) soda water.

YIELD: 1 CUP (200 ML)

---

10 limes (for juice and zest)

1 cup (200 g) superfine (caster) sugar

Pinch of sea salt

1 teaspoon citric acid (optional)

(1) Peel and juice the limes.

(2) Combine the juice with superfine sugar, lime zest, sea salt, and citric acid in a saucepan over medium heat.

(3) Cook until sugar is dissolved. Stir occasionally.

(4) Strain through a coffee filter into a bottle.

(5) Store in the fridge for up to 2 weeks.

STAR FRUIT CORDIAL

A tropical-flavored cordial made with star fruit that is bright and complex in the range of sweet to sour. It recalls fruity and acidic flavors of grapefruit, pear, and pineapple, and finishes on a gentle floral note. Try it in Starry Flower (see page 56).

YIELD: 1 CUP (200 ML)

---

5 star fruits

½ cup (100 ml) water

1 cup (200 g) superfine (caster) sugar

(1) Blend star fruits, water, and superfine sugar at high speed.

(2) Filter twice with a coffee filter in a bottle.

(3) Store it in the fridge for up to a week.

TOMATO CORDIAL

A different way to use tomatoes in your drinks, manipulating the acidity of the fruit and turning in a sweet component. It still conserves its original flavor but in a more delicate way. Use it in Basil Rosé Spritz (see page 108).

YIELD: 1 CUP (200 ML)

---

1 ½ cups (200 g) cherry tomatoes

1:1 superfine (caster) sugar (the same amount of juice you will get after you blend cherry tomatoes)

1 teaspoon malic solution

(1) Blitz cherry tomatoes in a blender at medium speed until you get a smooth texture.

(2) Filter twice through a muslin cloth in order to keep the juice and remove the flesh.

(3) In a saucepan over medium heat, combine the juice and superfine sugar (weigh the juice and add the same amount of sugar). Stir until dissolved.

(4) Remove the saucepan from the heat and let the juice cool down.

(5) Weigh the cordial obtained and combine it with malic solution.

(6) Mix until it's dissolved.

(7) Store it in the fridge for up to 6 days.

WATERMELON CORDIAL

A very easy cordial to make that saves some space in the fridge when you have a leftover watermelon. You can use it in Bellini in Vacation (see page 111) or in a watermelon Flora Dora.

YIELD: 1¼ CUPS (300 ML)

---

1 ¼ cups (300 ml) watermelon juice

1 ½ cups (300 g) super-fine (caster) sugar

(1) In a saucepan over medium heat, combine watermelon juice and superfine sugar.

(2) Cook until sugar is dissolved, stirring occasionally.

(3) Remove from heat and let it cool down.

(4) Strain into a bottle and store it in the fridge for up to 2 weeks.

• INFUSIONS •

The infusion process has gained popularity in recent years, but it is an ancient practice. It is a simple process, whereby you combine the spirit with fruit, herbs, or other ingredients in a jar to infuse them. Leave some air space at the top since you need to shake it. Keep the jar in a dark place and shake it daily. Remember to taste the spirit once a day after the first 24 hours and twice a day if you are using a strong flavor ingredient, such as jalapeño. The average time of infusion is between 2 and 5 days, and once ready, you need to double strain through a muslin cloth or coffee filter into a bottle, preventing the small particles from falling in.

APPLE SKIN-INFUSED DRY ROSÉ WINE

A fruity infusion with a light apple note that you can use in Apple & Saffron Spritz (see page 33) and in a London Calling. Do not waste the apples. Eat them in a fruit salad or make a delicious pie. You will have a pudding and a cocktail that will match perfectly.

YIELD: 13 ½ OUNCES (400 ML)

---

6 apples skins

13 ½ ounces (400 ml) dry rosé wine

(1) Wash and peel six apples.

(2) Combine peels and dry rosé wine in a jar (or vacuum bag) and seal it. Shake to mix, and let rest for 72 hours.

(3) Strain through a muslin cloth or fine-mesh strainer into a bottle, cover, and store in the fridge for up to 1 week.

BLOOD ORANGE PEELS-INFUSED SWEET ROSÉ

A zesty infusion with orange notes. You can use it in Rusty Stone Blood (see page 100) or in a Spritz. You can use any oranges you like, but the blood oranges are juicier and have a more intense flavor.

YIELD: 6 ⅔ OUNCES (200 ML)

---

3 blood orange peels, piths removed

6 ⅔ ounces (200 ml) sweet rosé wine

(1) Combine orange peels and sweet rosé wine in a vacuum bag or a jar.

(2) Let it rest in the fridge for 24 hours.

(3) Strain into a bottle and store in the fridge for up to 6 days.

FAVA BEANS-INFUSED VODKA

Light, sweet vegetable notes with a buttery and nutty finish. Use it in Rosé Crush (see page 91)—it will be delicious.

YIELD: 11 ⅔ OUNCES (350 ML)

---

2 ½ ounces (70 g) fava beans, shells and outer skins removed

11 ⅔ ounces (350 ml) vodka

(1) Combine fava beans and vodka in a vacuum bag or a jar.

(2) Seal and let rest at room temperature for 24 hours.

(3) Strain through a coffee filter in a bottle.

(4) Store at room temperature for up to 3 months.

FENNEL SEEDS-INFUSED TEQUILA

Fennel brings an anise note to tequila, with a strong herbal flavor and a slight bitter perfume on the nose. Try it in Rosé & Melon Fizz (see page 46).

YIELD: 10 OUNCES (300 ML)

---

10 ounces (300 ml) tequila

1 ½ teaspoon (7 g) fennel seeds

(1) Give the fennel seeds a slight press: bash on a dry chopping board with the flat part of a knife.

(2) Combine them with tequila in a jar and let rest for 2 hours at room temperature.

(3) Fine strain and bottle it.

(4) Store at room temperature for up to 3 months.

PARSNIP-INFUSED WHITE RUM

Vegetable notes and savory flavors to add to your rum. Try in Rosé Roots (see page 99).

YIELD: 11 ⅔ OUNCES (350 ML)

---

4 parsnips

11 ⅔ ounces (350 ml) white rum

(1) Cut parsnips into small chunks and roast them in the oven for 30 minutes at 300°F (150°C).

(2) Once roasted, let them cool down and combine with rum in a jar or vacuum bag.

(3) Place in the fridge for 24 hours.

(4) Strain into a bottle and store in the fridge for up to 2 weeks.

PASSION FRUIT-INFUSED ROSÉ

A great way to extract passion fruit flavors to infuse in rosé wine, highlighting the fruity side of the wine. It can be used in Passiony (see page 41).

YIELD: 10 OUNCES (300 ML)

---

3 passion fruits

10 ounces (300 ml) rosé wine

(1) Combine passion fruits and rosé wine in a vacuum bag.

(2) Seal and sous vide for two hours at 140°F (60°C).

(3) Filter twice through a coffee filter into a bottle.

(4) Store in the fridge for up to 2 weeks.

For the sous vide technique, just attach a precision cooker to a pot of water and set the time and temperature. Then, seal the bag and clip it into the inside of the pot.

RASPBERRIES-INFUSED DRY ROSÉ

A delicious fruity and sour infusion that will bring tannin and brightness to drinks. Use it in Jalisco Spritzer and in a Roseberry Romance (see page 113 and 49).

YIELD: 6 ⅔ OUNCES (200 ML)

---

6 ⅔ ounces (200 ml) dry rosé

10 fresh raspberries, washed

(1) Seal raspberries and dry rosé in a vacuum bag.

(2) Place in the fridge for 24 hours.

(3) Remove it and strain the liquid into a bottle.

(4) Store in the fridge for up to 5 days.

SPICED ROSÉ WINE

A very intense combination of flavors with the refreshing notes from orange peel. Use it in classic cocktails, such as a low-ABV Dark'n'Stormy or a low-ABV Cuba Libre. Also try it out in Rosé Jungle Bird (see page 53).

YIELD: 11 ⅔ OUNCES (350 ML)

---

8 ¾ ounces (250 ml) rosé wine

3 ⅓ ounces (100 ml) dark rum

1 vanilla pod

2 orange peels, piths removed

1 teaspoon cloves

1 cinnamon stick

½ teaspoon nutmeg powder

(1) Combine rosé wine, dark rum, vanilla pod, orange peels, cloves, cinnamon stick, and nutmeg powder in a vacuum bag.

(2) Let it rest at room temperature for 12 hours. Shake it occasionally.

(3) Strain through a coffee filter into a bottle.

(4) Store in the fridge for up to a month.

STRAWBERRIES-INFUSED VODKA

A fruity infusion you can play around with. You can use it in different cocktails, such as a classic Kamikaze (use the infused vodka instead of the tequila) or in a Floating Leaf (see page 116).

YIELD: 6 ⅔ OUNCES (200 ML)

---

6 ⅔ ounces (200 ml) vodka

10 strawberries, washed

(1) Cut strawberries in half and place them with vodka in a vacuum bag.

(2) Place the vacuum bag in a sous vide at 140°F (60°C) for 1 hour.

(3) Let it cool down and strain into a bottle.

(4) Store in the fridge for up to 3 months.

For the sous vide technique, you just need to attach a precision cooker to a pot of water and set the time and temperature, seal the ingredients into a bag, and clip it to the inside of the pot.

TOASTED CORIANDER
SEEDS-INFUSED
DRY ROSÉ

A sharp and lemony infusion with an herb aftertaste and a sweet smell.
Use it in Tropical Rosé Rain (see page 62)—it will be delicious.

YIELD: 10 OUNCES (300 ML) DRY ROSÉ

⅓ cup (20 g) coriander seeds

10 ounces (300 ml) dry rosé

(1) In a saucepan over medium heat, toast coriander seeds until they start to brown.

(2) Once toasted, combine them with dry rosé wine in a jar.

(3) Let rest at room temperature for 3 hours.

(4) Strain into a bottle and store in the fridge for 1 week.

TOASTED ALMOND FLOUR-INFUSED TEQUILA

An infusion with a strong nutty flavor on the nose but a very delicate almond note on the palate. Use it in Rosé Attraction (see page 88) or in a classic Jalisco Espresso.

YIELD: 10 OUNCES (300 ML)

---

1 ½ tablespoons (10 g) almond flour

10 ounces (300 ml) tequila

(1) In a saucepan over medium heat, toast almond flour until it browns in color. Keep stirring it; otherwise, it will burn.

(2) Once almond flour is toasted, combine it with tequila in a jar.

(3) Let it rest for 15 minutes, and then strain through a coffee filter into a bottle.

(4) Store in the fridge for up to 6 months.

TOASTED WALNUT-INFUSED WHISKEY

A rich infusion with nutty notes that works very well with bourbon. Use it in a Walnut Whiskey Sour or in Walnut & Plum Highball (see page 57).

YIELD: 11 ⅔ OUNCES (350 ML)

½ cup (60 g) walnuts

11 ⅔ ounces (350 ml) whiskey

(1) Crush walnuts into small pieces and place them in a vacuum bag with whiskey.

(2) Seal, and sous vide for 3 hours at 140°F (60°C).

(3) Strain into a bottle and store in the fridge for up to a month.

For the sous vide technique, you just need to attach a precision cooker to a pot of water and set the time and temperature, seal the ingredients into a bag, and clip it to the inside of the pot.

VANILLA PODS-INFUSED BOURBON

A very pronounced vanilla flavor, buttery and rich too, that you can use in a classic Old Fashioned or Peach & Cocoa Wisher (see page 80). You can infuse vanilla pods in other spirits as well, just choose the one that you like the most.

YIELD: 11 ⅔ OUNCES (350 ML)

---

11 ⅔ ounces (350 ml) bourbon

3 vanilla pods

(1) Combine bourbon and vanilla pods in a vacuum bag.

(2) Seal and sous vide for two hours at 150°F (65°C).

(3) Strain through a coffee filter into a bottle and store at room temperature for 3 months.

For the sous vide technique, you just need to attach a precision cooker to a pot of water and set the time and temperature, seal the ingredients into a bag, and clip it to the inside of the pot.

• JUICES & PUREES •

Juices are some of the most common ingredients in cocktails. But purees can be used as well; just remember to filter them to get rid of chunks.

GINGER JUICE

Whether you use it for cocktails, such as Rosé Penicillin (95), mocktails, or cooking recipes, ginger juice is very easy to make. Try adding it to your teas as well.

YIELD: ⅔ CUP (150 ML)

---

2 cups (200 g) ginger root, about ½ to 1 inch per chunk

(1) Wash and dry ginger root, removing the bruised parts (otherwise, you can peel it if you prefer).

(2) Cut the roots into small chunks and place them in a blender.

(3) Blend for 2 minutes or until you get a pasty pulp.

(4) Strain the liquid through a muslin cloth into a jar or bottle and cover it. Store in the fridge for up to 2 weeks.

MELON JUICE

If you can't find it in the store, you can make it at home. A delicious drink you can have by itself or add in Rosé & Melon Fizz (see page 46).

YIELD: 1 ½ CUPS (350 ML)

---

2 cups (300 g) melon cantaloupe

¾ cup (175 ml) water

(1) Blend melon cantaloupe and water at high speed until you get a smooth juice.

(2) Strain through a coffee filter or muslin cloth into a bottle.

(3) Store in the fridge for up to 4 days.

MELON PUREE

Very versatile, you can make Melon Champagne Cocktail (see page 120) or use to make a twist on a Bellini. Instead of peach puree, pour in a shake 3 ounces (90 ml) prosecco rosé, ¹/₃ ounce (10 ml) lemon juice, 1 ²/₃ ounces (50 ml) melon puree, and ¹/₃ ounce (10 ml) simple syrup 2:1 (see page 166). Stir for 17 to 20 seconds and pour into a chilled flute. You will be amazed!

YIELD: 1 CUP (200 ML)

---

2 cups (300 g) melon cantaloupe, cut into pieces

½ cup (100 ml) water

(1) Blend melon cantaloupe and water at high speed until you get a smooth texture.

(2) Strain through a coffee filter into a bottle.

(3) Store in the fridge for up to 3 days.

PEACH PUREE

A fruity puree that you can use in a classic Bellini, or in Peachy Rosé Sour (see page 83). If you are in a rush, you can buy peach juice but remember to filter it twice through a coffee filter before adding it to the drink. This will help to make a smooth drink, instead of having chunks in the glass.

YIELD: 1 CUP (200 ML)

---

4 peaches,
washed

½ cup (100 ml)
water

(1) Blend peaches at high speed until you get a smooth texture and add the water.

(2) Filter twice through a coffee filter to keep the juice and remove the flesh.

(3) Bottle it and store in the fridge for up to 5 days.

REDUCTIONS & SYRUPS

Reduction is when you reduce a quantity of a liquid to amplify the flavors.
The result will be thicker and will give more texture to cocktails as well.
Syrups are very easy to make, and they are essentials behind the
bar. They are always made with 1 part water and 1 part sugar.
You simply need to dissolve sugar in water. There are unlimited
flavored syrups, and some are more complex than others.

BASIL SYRUP

*Basil syrup is great for summer cocktails, such as a classic Gimlet or
Floating Leaf (see page 116). It is very versatile and can be used for
mocktails too.*

YIELD: 1 ¼ CUPS (300 ML)

---

20 fresh basil leaves

1 ¼ cups (300 ml) water

**1 ½ cups (300 g) superfine
(caster) sugar**

(1) Bring water to a boil over high
heat.

(2) Remove from heat and combine
boiling water with basil.

(3) Let it steep for 10 minutes. Then
stir in sugar until it is dissolved.

(4) Cool and strain into a bottle.
Cover and store in the fridge for up to
3 months.

CHILI TINCTURE

A tincture is a spirit infused with spices, herbs, fruits, flowers, or vegetables. It is usually made in small batches, since you just need a few drops per cocktail. Use a dropper bottle to pour it into the cocktail so that you will have more control. Try it in Rosé Crush (see page 91).

YIELD: 3 ⅓ OUNCES (100 ML)

---

3 ⅓ ounces (100 ml) over-proof spirit

2 bird's eye chili peppers, washed

(1) Cut chili peppers in half and remove any seeds.

(2) Combine chili peppers and over-proof spirit into a jar and seal it.

(3) Let it rest for 1 week at room temperature. Shake the jar occasionally. Strain into a bottle. Store at room temperature for up to 1 month.

If you want, you can quickly bring out the essential oils by toasting chili peppers and spices in a dry pan before infusing. You can use any type of chili pepper you like, according to how intense you want the flavor. Try it in Rosé Crush (see page 91).

CUCUMBER SYRUP

A refreshing and light syrup, perfect for hot summer days. Use it in Cucumber & Rosé Highball (see page 71) or in mocktails. Just add it to soda or tonic water to make delicious soft drinks.

YIELD: 1 ¼ CUPS (300 ML)

---

2 cucumber peels

1 ¼ cups (300 ml) water

1 ½ cups (300 g) superfine (caster) sugar

(1) Combine cucumber peels with water and superfine sugar in a saucepan over medium heat.

(2) Cook until sugar is dissolved.

(3) Strain through a coffee filter into a bottle and store in the fridge for up to a week.

Bartender's Tips: Do not waste the peeled cucumbers. Add them to a Greek-style feta salad to enjoy while sipping a Cucumber & Rosé Highball (see page 71).

GINGER SYRUP

Ginger Syrup is a very versatile ingredient. Use it in cooking or to give an extra spiced flavor to your cocktails. It will be great in Palomito, Spiced Rosé, and Spiced Summer Bowl (see pages 38, 103 and 127).

To make ginger syrup, follow the recipe for ginger juice, and start from there.

YIELD: 6 ⅔ OUNCES (200 ML)

---

1 cup (200 ml) ginger juice (see page 147)

1 cup (200 g) superfine (caster) sugar

(1) Combine ginger juice and superfine sugar in a saucepan over medium-high heat, stirring until sugar is dissolved.

(2) Strain into a bottle, cover, and store in the fridge for up to 2 weeks.

GRENADINE

Grenadine is a brilliant red pomegranate syrup. It is sweet and tart, and you can use it in many recipes or substitute it for simple syrup. Use it for Clementé Soda, Labirinto, Lychee Rosé Martini, and French Rosé Cocktail (see pages 68, 75, 76, and 115), or a Shirley Temple mocktail. Store it in the fridge for up to 3 weeks.

YIELD: 1 CUP (200 ML)

---

1 cup (200 ml)
pomegranate juice

1 cup (200 g)
superfine (caster)
sugar

(1) In a saucepan, combine pomegranate juice and sugar.

(2) Bring it to a slow boil and stir constantly until sugar is dissolved.

(3) Reduce heat and cover the saucepan with a lid.

(4) Simmer for 15 to 20 minutes, stirring occasionally.

(5) Remove from heat and let it cool down.

(6) Strain into a bottle.

HONEY WATER

A lighter, smoother, and less-sweet version of honey. Try it in Walnut &
Plum Highball (see page 57), but also in teas. Or you can freeze it in an
ice cube tray and then add the honey cube to your drinks.

YIELD: 8 ½ OUNCES (250 ML)

**⅔ cup (200 ml)
honey**

**½ cup (100 ml)
boiling hot water**

(1) In a jar, combine honey and hot water.

(2) Stir until it gets smooth and well mixed.

(3) Strain through a muslin cloth into a bottle, cover
it, and store in the fridge for up to 1 month.

PASSION FRUIT SYRUP

A versatile syrup that you can use in many drinks. Try it in a classic Porn Star Martini or in Tropical Rosé Rain (see page 62).

YIELD: 1 CUP (200 ML)

---

1 cup (200 ml) passion fruit juice

1 cup (200 g) superfine (caster) sugar

(1) In a saucepan over medium heat, combine passion fruit juice and sugar.

(2) Stir until the sugar is dissolved.

(3) Strain into a bottle and store in the fridge for up to 2 weeks.

PEACH SYRUP

A very easy prep to make at home. You can use it in Spiced Rosé (see page 158), a Peach Margarita, or Peach Spritz.

YIELD: 1 CUP (200 ML)

---

2 peaches

1 cup (200 ml) water

½ cup (100 g) superfine (caster) sugar

(1) Cut peaches and roast them in the oven for 30 minutes at 320°F (160°C).

(2) Once roasted, blend them at high speed.

(3) Combine the juice obtained from peaches with water and superfine sugar in a saucepan.

(4) Cook on medium heat until sugar is dissolved. Stir occasionally.

(5) Strain into a bottle and store in the fridge for up to 1 week.

RASPBERRY SYRUP

A delicious syrup to use in your cocktails, such as Rosé Fountain (see page 51), but also on ice cream or pancakes!

YIELD: 1 CUP (200 ML)

---

1 ½ cups (150 g) raspberries

1 cup (200 ml) water

1 cup (200 g) superfine (caster) sugar

(1) Combine raspberries with water and sugar in a saucepan over medium heat, stirring occasionally.

(2) Bring to a boil, or cook until the sugar is dissolved. (The longer you simmer, the thicker the syrup will be.) Remove from heat and let it cool down.

(3) Strain the liquid into a bottle. Cover and store in the fridge for up to 3 weeks.

ROSÉ HONEY

This syrup is rich in flavor and very easy to make. It's so versatile that you can use it in a classic Bee's Knees or in a Business Cocktail. Otherwise, try it in Rosé Penicillin and Rosé Pisco Sour (see pages 95 and 96).

YIELD: 1 ¼ CUPS (300 ML)

⅞ cup (300 g) honey

3 ⅓ ounces (100 ml) rosé wine

(1) In a saucepan over medium heat, combine honey and rosé wine.

(2) Cook until you get a smooth texture.

(3) Strain into a bottle and store in the fridge for up to 2 weeks.

ROSÉ REDUCTION (DRY, SWEET, AND SPARKLING)

This is an intriguing way to get more intense flavor out of rosé. Plus, if your rosé is going off, a reduction will be a great solution. Try the sweet rosé wine reduction in Plum Rosé (see page 84). Otherwise, you can try it with a dry or sparkling rosé and use it in Floating Leaf (see page 116).

YIELD: 10 OUNCES (300 ML)

---

10 ounces (300 ml) dry/sweet/sparkling rosé

⅓ cup (70 g) superfine (caster) sugar

(1) In a saucepan over medium-high heat, cook rosé wine until you get a reduction of 40%.

(2) Combine sugar and stir until it is dissolved.

(3) Let it cool down and strain into a bottle.

(4) Store in the fridge for up to 3 weeks.

ROSÉ WINE AND ROASTED PEACH SYRUP

A sweet and caramelized syrup which comes from the roasted peach and a touch of sweet rosé wine. A very delicious treat that you can use in Peach & Cocoa Wisher (see page 80).

YIELD: 1 CUP (200 ML)

---

4 peaches

1:1 superfine (caster) sugar (the amount of juice you will get after you blend peaches)

3 ⅓ ounces (100 ml) rosé wine

(1) Cut peaches and roast them in the oven for 30 minutes at 320°F (160°C).

(2) Once roasted, blend them at high speed.

(3) Weigh the juice obtained from peaches and combine it with the same amount of sugar and rosé wine.

(4) Cook until sugar is dissolved. Stir occasionally.

(5) Strain through a coffee filter into a bottle and store in the fridge for up to 6 days.

ROSÉ WINE SYRUP

This is a good way to save your wine when it is going off. Just make a syrup and use it as an ingredient of your cocktails, such as Gimlé, Rosé Attraction, and Labirinto (see pages 37, 88, and 75). You can use any wine you like. The flavor will be slightly different according to the wine you use, but it will still be a sweet syrup.

YIELD: 6 ⅔ OUNCES (200 ML)

---

6 ⅔ ounces (200 ml) sweet or dry rosé wine

2 cups (400 g) superfine (caster) sugar

(1) Combine sweet or dry rosé wine and sugar in a saucepan over medium heat.

(2) Cook until sugar is dissolved, stirring occasionally.

(3) Bottle and store in the fridge for up to 3 months.

ROSEMARY SYRUP

An herbal syrup that you can use in Summer Garden N.1 (see page 58). You can use any herbs you like, just follow the recipe, and you will have a wonderful selection of syrups for use in the kitchen, in your drinks, and as gifts as well.

YIELD: 1 ¼ CUPS (300 ML)

---

1 ¼ cups (300 ml) water

1 ½ cups (300 g) superfine (caster) sugar

7 rosemary sprigs

(1) Combine water, sugar, and rosemary sprigs in a saucepan over medium heat.

(2) Cook until sugar is dissolved, stirring occasionally.

(3) Let it cool down and strain into a bottle through a coffee filter.

(4) Store in the fridge for up to a week.

SAFFRON HONEY

A sweet and intense honey that you can use in a Bee's Knees or in Apple & Saffron Spritz (see page 33). Saffron enriches the flavor and gives the honey a brilliant color. The ratio is 3:1 because the syrup will have more body and still keep a persistent honey flavor.

YIELD: 1 ½ CUPS (350 G)

---

1 cup (340 g) honey

½ cup (100 ml) hot water

¼ teaspoon (0.25 g) saffron threads

(1) In a jar, combine honey and hot water.

(2) Mix with a spoon until it's smooth.

(3) Keep stirring while you add saffron.

(4) Let it rest for 2 days at room temperature.

(5) Bottle it and store at room temperature for up to 3 months.

SIMPLE SYRUP 2:1

Whether you buy it, or you make your own (highly recommended), sugar syrup is one of those ingredients that you should always have in your home bar. The ratio I chose will give more texture to your cocktails.

YIELD: 1 CUP (200 ML)

---

1 cup (200 ml)
water

2 cups (400 g)
superfine (caster)
sugar

(1) Combine water and sugar in a jar, and stir until sugar is dissolved.

(2) Strain into a bottle and store in the fridge for up to 6 months (if you make a big batch).

STRAWBERRIES SYRUP

This recipe can save your strawberries from going bad. It lasts longer and saves space in the fridge. You can use it to make delicious cocktails, such as Pink Strawberry Rosé and Red Glass on a Highway (see pages 123 and 42), or pour on ice cream and pancakes—it will be delicious!

YIELD: 1 CUP (200 ML)

½ cup (100 g) strawberries, washed and cut into small pieces

1 cup (200 ml) water

1 cup (200 g) superfine (caster) sugar

(1) Place cut strawberries in a saucepan and cover them with water and sugar.

(2) Cook over medium heat, occasionally stirring, until the sugar is dissolved (at least 20 minutes).

(3) Let it cool, then strain through a muslin cloth or fine-mesh strainer into a bottle.

(4) Store in the fridge for up to 3 weeks.

SWEET ROSÉ AND STRAWBERRY SYRUP

A sweet and fruity syrup to use in Fruity Bag (see page 72). But here is a tip: try to spice up a strawberry cake with this syrup! You will be amazed.

YIELD: 1 CUP (200 ML)

---

15 strawberries

1 cup (200 ml) water

1 cup (200 g) superfine (caster) sugar

(1) Combine strawberries with water and sugar in a saucepan over medium heat, stirring occasionally; bring to a boil or until the sugar is dissolved. (The longer you simmer, the thicker the syrup will be.) Remove from heat and let it cool down.

(2) Strain the liquid into a bottle. Cover and store in the fridge for up to 3 weeks.

You can also blend strawberries first and then combine them with water and caster sugar so that you will have a stronger flavor, and it will be faster to get a syrup.

TOASTED PINE NUTS SYRUP

A nutty syrup that brings a buttery texture to the cocktails, while adding a savory note as well. Try it in Roseberry Romance (see page 49).

YIELD: 1 CUP (200 ML)

¼ cup (30 g) pine nuts

1 cup (200 ml) water

1 cup (200 g) superfine (caster) sugar

(1) In a saucepan over medium heat, toast pine nuts until they brown in color.

(2) In a different saucepan over medium-high heat, combine water and sugar and stir until the sugar is dissolved.

(3) Once pine nuts are toasted, combine them with the sugar syrup on medium-high heat for 10 minutes, stirring occasionally.

(4) Let it cool down, and then strain it into a bottle.

(5) Store in the fridge for up to 3 months.

THYME SYRUP

An herbal syrup that will give a sweet, delicate note to your cocktails. And remember, you can make various syrups out of any herbs. Use thyme syrup in Rosé Roots (see page 99).

YIELD: 1 ¼ CUPS (300 ML)

---

1 ¼ cups (300 ml) water

1 ½ cups (300 g) superfine (caster) sugar

8 thyme sprigs

(1) Combine water, sugar, and thyme sprigs in a saucepan over medium heat.

(2) Cook until sugar is dissolved, stirring occasionally.

(3) Let it cool down and strain into a bottle through a coffee filter.

(4) Store it in the fridge for up to 1 week.

VANILLA SYRUP

A sweet and delicate recipe, so easy to make that you will stop buying vanilla syrup from the store. You can use it in many cocktails, such as Jalisco Spritzer and Rosé & Melon Fizz (see pages 113 and 46), and in your desserts too.

YIELD: 2 CUPS (500 ML)

---

2 cups (500 ml) water

2 ½ cups (500 g) superfine (caster) sugar

1 teaspoon (4 g) vanilla extract

(1) In a saucepan over medium heat, combine water and sugar, stirring occasionally for 10 minutes or until the sugar is dissolved. Remove from heat, let cool, and then stir in vanilla extract.

(2) Strain into a bottle and cover. It is now ready to use, or store in a cold, dry place for up to about 3 months, if not longer.

WITBIER (WHITE ALE) REDUCTION

Reduction gets the most flavor out of beers; add it to cocktails to get a rich flavor and texture. Try it in Tropical Rosé Rain (see page 62).

YIELD: 1 CUP (200 ML)

½ pint (200 ml) witbier (white ale)

1 cup (200 g) superfine (caster) sugar

(1) In a saucepan, combine beer and sugar.

(2) Cook on medium heat, stirring occasionally, until sugar is dissolved.

(3) Let it cool down and strain into a bottle. Cover and store in the fridge for up to 1 week.

• SODAS •

To make a soda at home, get a siphon and add a soda charger. It's very easy, and you can make tasty sodas to add to your cocktails or use as mocktails.

MANGO SODA

A refreshing tropical soda to add to Rosmango Fizz (see page 50). Try it on its own as well—it's delicious.

YIELD: DEPENDS ON THE QUANTITY OF JUICE YOU GET

---

8 mangos
3:1 water

(1) Cut mangos into small pieces.

(2) Blend at high speed until you get a smooth texture.

(3) Filter through a coffee filter into a jar.

(4) Weigh out the juice and combine it with water to the ratio of 3 parts mango juice to 1 part water.

(5) Bottle it and store in the fridge for 12 hours.

(6) Pour into a siphon and charge it with a soda charger.

With a Thermomix

(1) Wash and cut mangos.

(2) Combine flesh and Pectinex into the Thermomix and blitz at 130°F (55°C) at speed 4 for 16 minutes.

(3) Pass through a coffee filter.

With the acidity of the Pectinex, you will get a clarified juice and more ratio of juice because Pectinex helps to separate the flesh from the juice.

PLUM SODA

This soda is sweet and light, very refreshing, and suitable for kids and adults. You can drink it by itself, or you can use it in cocktails, such as a Walnut & Plum Highball (see page 57).

YIELD: DEPENDS ON THE QUANTITY OF JUICE YOU GET

---

15 plums

3:1 water

(1) Wash plums and cut them into small pieces.

(2) Blend at high speed until you get a smooth texture.

(3) Filter through a coffee filter in a jar.

(4) Weigh out the juice and combine it with water to the ratio of 3 parts plum juice to 1 part water.

(5) Bottle it and store in the fridge for 12 hours.

(6) Pour into a siphon and charge it with a soda charger.

If you have a Thermomix, follow the same recipe for mango soda (see page 173).

ABOUT THE AUTHOR

Emanuele Mensah is a mixologist, bar manager, photographer, and videographer based in London. He has worked for some of the best cocktail bars in the world, including Disrepute in London and Eau-de-Vie Sydney, and he was named one of the World Class Top 100 Bartenders by Diageo Reserve. On Instagram and YouTube, you can find him at Cocktails with Lele (@CocktailsWithLele), where he shows how to make excellent classic cocktails in a home bar. He teaches complex techniques as well as the basics and shares classic cocktail recipes, craft concoctions, plus innovative creations of his own.

Lele is all about sustainability and applies a zero-waste policy to his ideas and concepts; everything has a purpose and must be used. He believes in interpreting cocktails with a fresh perspective, while taking inspiration from drinks and drink recipes from the past. This means returning to the original purpose of spirits when they were used medicinally, in the mezcal of Oaxaca and around the world.

He feels that drinking a cocktail should be a moment of pleasure and sharing.

ABOUT CIDER MILL PRESS BOOK PUBLISHERS

Good ideas ripen with time. From seed to harvest, Cider Mill Press brings fine reading, information, and entertainment together between the covers of its creatively crafted books. Our Cider Mill bears fruit twice a year, publishing a new crop of titles each spring and fall.

"Where Good Books Are Ready for Press"

501 Nelson Place
Nashville, Tennessee 37214

cidermillpress.com